C MINIMANUAL WITH C++ SUPPLEMENT

to Accompany Appleby:
Programming Languages:
Paradigm and Practice

Also available from McGraw-Hill

SCHAUM'S OUTLINE SERIES IN COMPUTERS

Most outlines include basic theory, definitions, and hundreds of solved problems and supplementary problems with answers. Titles on the current list include:

Advanced Structured Cobol
Boolean Algebra
Computer Graphics
Computer Science
Computers and Business
Computers and Programming
Data Processing
Data Structures
Digital Principles, 2d edition
Discrete Mathematics
Essential Computer Mathematics
Linear Algebra, 2d edition
Mathematical Handbook of Formulas & Tables
Matrix Operations
Microprocessor Fundamentals, 2d edition
Programming with Advanced Structured Cobol
Programming with Assembly Language
Programming with Basic, 2d edition
Programming with C
Programming with Fortran
Programming with Pascal
Programming with Structured Cobol

SCHAUM'S SOLVED PROBLEMS BOOKS

Each title in this series is a complete and expert source of solved problems containing thousands of problems with worked out solutions. Related titles on the current list include:

3000 Solved Problems in Calculus
2500 Solved Problems in Differential Equations
2000 Solved Problems in Discrete Mathematics
3000 Solved Problems in Linear Algebra
2000 Solved Problems in Numerical Analysis

Available at your College Bookstore. A complete listing of Schaum titles may be obtained by writing to: Schaum Division
McGraw-Hill, Inc.
Princeton Road, S-1
Hightstown, NJ 08520

C MINIMANUAL WITH C++ SUPPLEMENT

to Accompany Appleby: Programming Languages: Paradigm and Practice

Maryam Shayegan Hastings
with a chapter on C++ by
William W. Hastings

McGraw-Hill, Inc.
New York St. Louis San Francisco Auckland Bogotá Caracas Hamburg
Lisbon London Madrid Mexico Milan Montreal New Delhi Paris
San Juan São Paulo Singapore Sydney Tokyo Toronto

C MiniManual with C++ Supplement to Accompany Appleby: Programming Languages: Paradigm and Practice

Copyright © 1991 by McGraw-Hill, Inc. All rights reserved. Printed in the United States of America. Except as permitted under the United States Copyright Act of 1976, no part of this publication may be reproduced or distributed in any form or by any means, or stored in a data base or retrieval system, without the prior written permission of the publisher.

1 2 3 4 5 6 7 8 9 0 DOC DOC 9 0 9 8 7 6 5 4 3 2 1

ISBN 0-07-002576-2

This book was designed and electronically typeset in Palatino
and Univers by Ocean View Technical Publications.
The editor was Eric M. Munson;
the production supervisor was Annette Mayeski.
Cover design was done by Terry Earlywine;
copyediting was done by P. J. Schemenauer;
text programming was done by Bruce Boston and Brooke Nicholson.
The index was prepared by Mark Savage.
Project supervision was done by Business Media Resources.
R. R. Donnelley & Sons Company was printer and binder.

Trademarked products cited:
The version of C described in this manual is the new ANSI Standard C
IBM PC 8086 and IBM PC are trademarks of the International Business Machines
　　Corporation
Turbo C, Turbo C++, Turbo C Editor, and Turbo Debugger are trademarks of Borland
　　International
MS-DOS is a registered trademark of Microsoft Corporation
Ada is a registered trademark of the U.S. Government, Ada Joint Program Office
UNIX is a trademark of AT&T
VAX is a trademark of Digital Equipment Corporation

To my mother and father

CONTENTS

PREFACE   xi

1   A PROGRAM IN C   1

2   SIMPLE DATA TYPES AND OPERATIONS   3
    2.1   VARIABLE NAMES   3
    2.2   SIMPLE DATA TYPES   3
           Integer Types   4
           Floating (Real) Types   4
           char (Character)   6
    2.3   BINARY ARITHMETIC OPERATORS   6
    2.4   UNARY ARITHMETIC OPERATORS   7
    2.5   INTEGER ARITHMETIC   7
    2.6   FLOATING-POINT ARITHMETIC   8
    2.7   RELATIONAL OPERATORS   8
    2.8   LOGICAL OPERATORS   8
    2.9   BIT OPERATIONS   9
    2.10   TYPE CASTS   10

3   CONTROL STRUCTURES   13
    3.1   THE if STATEMENT   13
    3.2   THE if-else STATEMENT   13
    3.3   THE NESTED if   14
    3.4   THE switch STATEMENT   15
    3.5   THE CONDITIONAL EXPRESSION OPERATOR   17
    3.6   LOOPING   17
           The for Loop   17
           The break Statement   18
           The continue Statement   19
           The while Loop   19
           The do-while Loop   21
    3.7   THE goto STATEMENT   21

4 POINTERS, ARRAYS AND STRUCTURES 23

    4.1   POINTERS   23
    4.2   INITIALIZING ARRAYS   26
    4.3   CHARACTER STRINGS   26
    4.4   ENUMERATED TYPES   26
    4.5   STRUCTURES   28
    4.6   UNIONS   29
    4.7   SIZEOF OPERATOR   31
    4.8   MULTIDIMENSIONAL ARRAYS   32

5 FUNCTIONS 35

    5.1   FUNCTION FORMAT   35
    5.2   PARAMETER LIST   36
    5.3   RETURN TYPE   37
    5.4   FUNCTION PROTOTYPES   37
    5.5   FUNCTION BODY   37
    5.6   STORAGE CLASSES   38
          Static and Auto Variables   38
          Global Variables   38
    5.7   SEPARATE COMPILATIONS AND EXTERNAL VARIABLES AND FUNCTIONS   39
    5.8   RECURSION   41

6 INPUT AND OUTPUT 43

    6.1   STANDARD I/O   43
    6.2   EXTERNAL FILES   47
          fprintf and fscanf   49
          fgets and fputs   49
    6.3   RANDOM ACCESS   49
    6.4   BINARY I/O   50

7 DYNAMIC DATA STRUCTURES 51

    7.1   typedef   51
    7.2   LINKED LISTS   52
    7.3   BINARY TREES   52

8 THE PREPROCESSOR 57

    8.1   MACRO DEFINITIONS   57
    8.2   FILE INCLUSION   59
    8.3   CONDITIONAL COMPILATION   59

9 TURBO C   61

- 9.1 THE MENU   61
  - *The File Menu*   61
  - *The Edit Command*   62
  - *The Run Menu*   62
  - *The Compile Menu*   63
  - *The Project Menu*   64
  - *The Options Menu*   64
  - *The Debug Menu*   64
  - *The Break/Watch Menu*   65
  - *A Debugging Session*   65
- 9.2 TURBO C CHARACTER GRAPHICS   67
  - *gotoxy, clrscr*   67
  - *Windows*   67

10 INTRODUCTION TO C++   71

- 10.1 CLASSES   71
- 10.2 CONSTRUCTORS   74
- 10.3 MEMBER FUNCTIONS OF CLASS FRACTION   74
- 10.4 PROPERTIES OF CLASSES   76
- 10.5 ANOTHER CLASS EXAMPLE   77
- 10.6 A DERIVED CLASS   79

A LANGUAGE DESCRIPTION   83

C TOKENS   83
INTEGER, FLOATING , CHARACTER CONSTANTS
AND STRING LITERALS   84
VALID OPERATOR   86
DECLARATION SYNTAX   86
FUNCTION DEFINITION   89

B THE ASCII CHARACTER SET   93

C OPERATOR PRECEDENCE   95

D C FUNCTIONS   97

E TURBO C HOT KEYS   105

F SOLUTIONS TO CHAPTER EXERCISES   107

CHAPTER 2   107
CHAPTER 3   108

CHAPTER 4   109
CHAPTER 5   113
CHAPTER 6   116
CHAPTER 7   118
CHAPTER 8   121
CHAPTER 9   121
CHAPTER 10   123

REFERENCES   139

INDEX   141

PREFACE

This minimanual is intended to provide the reader with all the information needed to begin writing C programs. It is not a complete text on C but rather a summary of essential constructs of C. No previous knowledge of C is assumed. It has been written in accordance with the new ANSI and ISO standard for the C language. All C programs were compiled using Borland's Turbo C™ Version 2.0, and a discussion of that environment is included. The last chapter by William Hastings is a short discussion of C++ using Borland's Turbo C++™ to compile the programs.

    This manual was developed as part of a series of manuals to accompany the text *Programming Languages: Paradigm and Practice* by Doris Appleby. In addition to these manuals, the text also contains labs in several languages including three labs in C. These manuals are intended to contain all that students need in order to perform these labs. The solutions to the labs will be available to the instructor.

    Each chapter includes some simple exercises. At the end of selected chapters, we have included some puzzles inspired by Alan Feurer's C puzzles. For more substantial C programs, the reader is referred to the C labs developed for inclusion in an instructor's manual accompanying Appleby's programming languages text.

    This manual can be used in conjunction with Appleby's programming text or independently. It can be used by students in any computer science course where C is used or as text for a short course in C.

1
A PROGRAM IN C

We start our discussion of the C language with a simple C program; Figure 1.1. If we enter two data items as input, we can expect the output; shown in Figure 1.2.

Program 1.1
```
/* This program will compute the average of two
 * integers entered by the user. */
#include <stdio.h>
main()
{
 int number_1,number_2;
 float average;

 printf("Enter two numbers.\n");
 scanf("%d%d", &number_1, &number_2);
 average=(number_1+number_2)/2.0;
 printf("The average of %d and", number_1);
 printf(" %d is\n Average=%.2f\n",number_2,average");
}
```

FIGURE 1.1 Program to calculate average

```
                        Enter two numbers
3 6
                        The average of 3 and 6 is
                        Average=4.50
sample input           output
```

FIGURE 1.2 Sample input and output produced by Program 1.1 in Figure 1.1

1

This program begins with a *comment*. Comments begin with the pair "/*" and end with the next occurrence of the pair "*/." A comment may appear anywhere a space is allowed. Following the opening comment is a "preprocessor directive," which will be discussed in subsequent chapters. (This directive provides information about I/O functions to the compiler.)

Every C program must contain the function `main`, where the program is to begin execution. All statements within the braces are part of the `main` function. The braces delimit a *block*, which is analogous to a compound statement delimited by BEGIN and END in Pascal. In this example the function `main` has no parameters since none are named between the parentheses following `main`. Other functions may appear before or after the `main` function.

Before variables are used in C, their type must be declared. The variable declarations appear at the beginning of a function. The variables number_1 and number_2 are of type int (integer) and average is of type `float` (a floating point or real number).

The first statement is a call to the library function `printf`, which simply prints out the prompt between the quotation marks. The characters "\n" tell the C system to go to a new line. The second and third calls to the function `printf` output numerical values according to the conversion specifications `%d` for an integer value and `%f` for a floating-point value. The specification `%.2f` indicates floating-point output with two places after the decimal point. There must be conversion specifications (in the correct order) for each argument after the format string. In the function call below, the `%d` is the conversion for number_2 and `%.2f` for the variable average.

```
printf(" %d is\nAverage=%.2f\n",number_2,average);
```

The second statement of our example program is a function call to the predefined function `scanf`, which enables the user to enter values into the program. The format strings for `scanf` are similar to those for `printf`. The `%d` indicates that the function is expecting an integer value to be input. In the call to `printf`, the name of the variable being output is used, but in scanf the address of the variable is passed to the function in order for the input data to be placed in the correct location. In C the "&" operator yields the *address* (or location) of a variable. Thus &number_1 is the address of the variable number_1. The following function call to `scanf` is expecting two integer values to be input for number_1 and number_2.

```
scanf("%d%d", &number_1, &number_2);
```

The assignment statement below uses parentheses to change the order of the evaluation. The order of arithmetic operations in C is the usual one.

```
average = (number_1 + number_2)/2.0;
```

Finally, note that all statements in C end with a semicolon.

2
SIMPLE DATA TYPES AND OPERATIONS

2.1 VARIABLE NAMES

We have seen two types of variables in the previous chapter. The variable number_1 was of type `int` and the variable average of type `float`. In C variable names must begin with a letter or an underscore(_) and may be any combination of upper or lower case letters, underscore, or the digits 0 through 9. There is no limit to the number of characters used in variable names, but only the first 31 characters are significant. In C upper and lower case letters are distinct, so that the variable AVERAGE and average are two different variables. Below is a list of valid and invalid variable names.

Valid	Invalid
number	3x2_matrix
first_number	long
_Total	second number
A_3x2_matrix	number_of_*s

The variable name 3x2_matrix starts with a digit; the word long is a keyword; the string "second number" contains a space and the string number_of_*s has the illegal character *.

2.2 SIMPLE DATA TYPES

C features three basic arithmetic data types: *integer*, *floating point* and *character*.

Integer Types

In C the basic integer type is `int`. This basic type may be modified by the qualifiers `short` or `long`. On personal computers a `short int` and an `int` are both usually two bytes, while a `long` is four bytes. Integer values are usually stored in variables of type `int`, unless their size requires the greater range of type `long`. Type `short int` (or even type `char`) may be used to save memory. The conversion specifiers used to display or read an `int`, `short int`, or `long int` are respectively %d, %hd and %ld. The following are some possible `short` and `long int` declarations.

```
long number_of_seconds;
short age;
```

Note that `short int`, for example, may be abbreviated `short`.

Any of these integer types may be further qualified by `signed` or `unsigned`. By default, an integer variable is signed; that is, it may hold both positive and negative values. An `unsigned` type may hold zero or a positive value. If a variable of type `int` occupies two bytes, then

```
int x;    /* -32768 <= x < 32768 */
unsigned y; /* 0 <= y < 65536 */
```

The conversion specifier for an `unsigned` value is %u (or %hu for `unsigned short` and %lu `unsigned long`).

In a C program an integer constant may be expressed in *octal*, that is, base 8, or in *hexadecimal*, that is, base 16. In octal notation the integer constant is preceded by 0 and the remaining digits must be between 0 and 7. For example, the octal constant 0167 represents the decimal value 119 (1 x 64 + 6 x 8 + 7). If an integer constant starts with 0 followed by the letter *x* (lower or upper case), the value is taken as hexadecimal. For example, the hexadecimal constant 0x4BE represents the decimal value 1,214 (4 x 256 + 11 x 16 + 14). The conversion specifier for an octal value using `printf` or `scanf` is %o, and for a hexadecimal, %x.

An integer constant has type `int` unless it is too large, in which case it has type `long` or (for very large positive constants) `unsigned long`. Adding the letters *L* and/or *U* (lower or upper case) to the end of the number changes the type to `long` and/or `unsigned`. For example, 1210UL is an `unsigned long` constant.

Floating (Real) Types

Real (floating-point) numbers in C have type `float`, `double` or `long double`. The number of bits devoted to the exponent and the fraction (mantissa) is dependent on the machine in use. There is always a sign bit. In expressing floating-point constants, digits before or after the decimal point may be omitted. The values .375, -0.468, and 34E-7 are all admissible floating-point constants. Constants are of type double unless the suffix *F* (float) or *L* (long double) is added. For example, 3.2E4F and 1e0L are of type float and long double respectively.

The type float uses the smallest number of bits (typically 32). To gain more accuracy and range in storing reals, the type double, or even long double, is used. The number of significant digits is typically increased from about 7 to about 17 with type double. The conversion specifiers for use with printf and scanf are %f, %lf, and %Lf for variables of type float, double and long double respectively. The scientific notation, such as in 2.45E13, may be used to display floating-point values using the %e (or %le or %Le) format. Program 2.1 in Figure 2.1 illustrates the arithmetic types.

Program 2.1
```
main ()
{
 int    i1 = -5,
        i2 = 70,
        i3 = 0x2b5;    /*hex 2b5, decimal 693*/
 long   l = 167454623; /* cannot be represented
                          in 16 bits*/
 unsigned int   u1 = 037,   /*octal 37, decimal 31*/
                u2 = -57;
 float f1 = .00578,
       f2 = -.024e-7;
 double d1 = 45.67894351e15;

 printf("i1 = %d , i2 = %d\n", i1,i2);
 printf("i3 = %x in hex, which is decimal %d\n", i3,i3);
 printf("l = %ld\n",l);
 printf("u1 = %o in octal, which is decimal %d\n", u1,u1);
 printf("u2 = %d, stored as unsigned int u2 = %u\n", u2,u2);
 printf("f1 = %f, f2 = %f\n",f1,f2);
 printf("d1 = %f = %e\n", d1,d1);
}
```

Program 2.1 output
```
i1 = -5 , i2 = 70
i3 = 2b5 in hex, which is decimal 693
l = 167454623
u1 = 37 in octal,  which is decimal 31
u2 = -57, stored as unsigned int u2 = 65479
f1 = 0.005780, f2 = -0.000000
d1 = 45678943510000000.000000 = 4.56789e+16
```

FIGURE 2.1 Program to demonstrate int, long, unsigned, float and double types

char (Character)

A variable of type `char` is used to store a single character. There are 128 *ASCII* (American Standard Code for Information Interchange) characters used by most computer systems. (See Appendix B for the listing of the ASCII characters.) Character constants are denoted by a single character in single quotes. To represent special characters such as the "newline" character, an *escape sequence* is used. An escape sequence begins with the backslash character and is followed by a single-character mnemonic, 1 to 3 octal digits, or the letter *x* followed by one or two hexadecimal digits.

The common mnemonics are the following:

`\"`	double quote
`\'`	single quote
`\\`	blackslash
`\f`	formfeed
`\n`	new line
`\t`	tab

(We encountered the escape sequence "\n" in Chapter 1.) The following are character constants (of type char): 'L', '#', '\'', '\t', '\0' (the null character), '\177', and '\x3A'.

```
putchar('\t');              /* output a tab */
end_of_line = (c == '\n');  /* Finished with line? */
```

Unlike strongly typed languages such as Pascal, the type `char` is one of the integer types in C, and, in particular, is compatible with type `int`. For example, if the value of the integer variable i is between 0 and 9, then the following assignment will convert it to the corresponding character:

```
c = i + '0';
```

When an integer value is converted to type `char`, the high-order (most significant) bits are lost.

2.3 BINARY ARITHMETIC OPERATORS

In C the `+` , `-` , `*` and `/` are the usual *binary operators*: add, subtract, multiply and divide. There is also the modulus operator (`%`) defined for integer types. The *modulus operator* gives the remainder of the first value divided by the second value. For example, `25 % 7 = 4` and `3 % 6 = 3`. When one of the arguments is negative, the result is implementation defined, although it must be true that

```
(A/B)*B + (A%B)
```

is equal to A (assuming B is not zero and no overflow occurs).

2.4 UNARY ARITHMETIC OPERATORS

There are three *unary arithmetic operators*; `-`, `--` and `++`. The `-` is the usual minus operator. The `++` operator increments the operand by one. For example:

```
b = d = 7;
a = ++b;   /* a and b are now both 8 */
c = d++;   /* d is 8, but c is 7 */
```

The *preincrement operator* (as in `++b`) increments its operand before its value is used in the rest of the expression, while the *postincrement operator* (as in `d++`) increments its operand after its value is used. The decrement operator `--` is analogous to the `++` operator. These operators may not be applied to floating-type operands.

The precedence of these operators is as follows: All unary operators are of the same precedence and are performed first. The `*`, `/`, and `%` are all of the same precedence and are performed after the unary operators. The binary operators `+` and `-` are performed next, and the *assignment operators* have lowest precedence. When two operators of the same precedence are encountered, they are performed left to right, except the assignment operators, which are performed right to left. For example:

```
b=5;
a = b += 4;   /* a and b are now 9 */
```

See Appendix C for a complete table of precedence rules.

The `+=` operator is a shorthand form combining the `=` and `+` operators. The same notation can be used for other operators. For example, `n *= m+2` is interpreted as n=(n) * (m+2).

2.5 INTEGER ARITHMETIC

All the operators above may be applied to operands of integer type, in which case the result is also of integer type. (Recall that the integer types include `char`, `short`, `int` and `long` — either `signed` or `unsigned`. In addition, bit fields and enumeration types, to be discussed later, are integer types.) In particular, integer division produces an integer result: 35 / 8 yields 4. The remainder is discarded.

The result of any integer expression is one of the four types: `int`, `unsigned int`, `long` or `unsigned long`. The rules determining which type is used are somewhat complicated, but may be summarized by saying that the result type is the first one among these four which can represent all possible values of the operand types.

2.6 FLOATING-POINT ARITHMETIC

Floating-point arithmetic is similar to other languages. The result type of an expression involving floating-point arguments is determined in a manner consistent with the rules for integer arithmetic. If one of the operands is of type `float` and the other is an integer type or type `float`, then the result will be of type `float`. Otherwise the result has type `double` or, if one of the operands is of type long double, `long double`. (In early versions of C, there was no type `long double`. Floating-point constants and the result of any arithmetic operation involving a floating type were always of type `double`.)

2.7 RELATIONAL OPERATORS

The *relational operators* are used to compare two arithmetic values. The result is either the value 1 ("true") or 0 ("false"). The expression a == b yields the value 1 if a equals b and 0 otherwise. The relation "not equal to" is !=. The other relational operators are <, >, <= and >=. These four operators all have the same precedence, which is higher than the == and the != operators and lower than the arithmetic operators (except the assignment operators).

2.8 LOGICAL OPERATORS

As for the relational operators, each *logical operator* yields 1 or 0. The operands are typically expressions containing a relational operator, but may be any arithmetic expression. Logical AND (&&) yields 1 if both operands are nonzero and 0 otherwise. Logical OR (||) returns 0 if both operands are zero and 1 otherwise. The ! returns 1 if the operand is zero and 1 otherwise. The logical AND operator has precedence over logical OR. The operands of a logical expression are evaluated from left to right until the result (1 or 0) of the entire expression can be determined. For example, the expression a||!b&&c is evaluated as a||((!b)&&c). If a is zero and b is not, then the value of the expression must be 0, and hence the value of c is not computed. Figure 2.2 illustrates these operators.

Program 2.2
```
main()
/*program to illustrate arithmetic, relational and logical operators*/
{
 int a=100, b=0, c=5, d=7,e;
 float r=2.5;
 printf("5 + 3 * a = %d\n", 5 + 3 * a);
 printf("a / r = %f\n",a/r);
 printf("a / 3 = %d ,but a / 3.0 = %5.2f\n", a/3, a/3.0);
 printf("a %% d = %d\n", a%d); /*Modulus operator*/
 printf("a %% c = %d\n",a%c);
 e = --c;
 printf("Decrement c and assign to e.");
 printf("  e = %d, c = %d\n",e,c);
 e = c--;
 printf("Assign c to e and decrement c.");
 printf("  e = %d, c = %d\n",e,c);
 if(a >= b && c < d)
   {
   printf("a is less than or equal to b and");
   printf(" c is less than d\n");
   }
 if(a == b || ! b)
   printf("a is equal to b or b is zero\n");
}
```

Program 2.2 Output
```
5 + 3 * a = 305
a / r = 40.000000
a / 3 = 33 ,but a / 3.0 = 33.33
a % d = 2
a % c = 0
Decrement c and assign to e.  e = 4, c = 4
Assign c to e and decrement c.  e = 4, c = 3
a is less than or equal to b and c is less than d
a is equal to b or b is zero
```

FIGURE 2.2 Program to illustrate the arithmetic, relational and logical operators

2.9 BIT OPERATIONS

C provides operations specifically designed for manipulating bits. *Bit operations* can be performed only on the integer types. There are five binary bit operations: the bitwise AND (&), the bitwise inclusive OR (|), the bitwise exclusive OR (^), the left shift (<<), and the right shift (>>). The following table shows the result of the first three binary bit operations as well as the unary bitwise NOT (~) for all possible values of bits b1 and b2.

b1	b2	b1 & b2	b1 | b2	b1 ^ b2	~b1
0	0	0	0	0	1
0	1	0	1	1	1
1	0	0	1	1	0
1	1	1	1	0	0

The bitwise AND operation can be used to mask bits, that is, to set certain bits in a word to zero. To clear (set to zero) all bits of w not in mask:

```
w = w & mask;
```

To set the second rightmost bit of w to 1:

```
w = w | 2;
```

To test if the second bit is set:

```
if ( (w & 2) != 0)
```

Note that we need the extra parentheses, since the relational operators have higher precedence than the bitwise AND and OR operators.

The bitwise shift operations shift an operand left or right by a specified number of bits. For example, for an `int`, w

```
w = w << 4;
```

shifts the bits of w 4 bits to the left. If w was 0...011101, then the left shift would result in w 0...0111010000.

Similarly, if w has the value 01..10011, then

```
w = w >> 2;
```

would result in a value of 0001..100 for w. (The result of a right shift applied to a negative quantity is implementation defined.)

We can examine a particular bit in a word w by combining the shift and AND operations. If we want to examine the rightmost nth bit, starting with the rightmost bit as the zero bit, then

```
nth_bit = (w >> n) & 1;
```

If w has the value 3, which is stored as 0..011, then the nth_bit would have the value 1 for n = 0 or 1 and zero for all other values of n. The value of n must be nonnegative and less than the number of bits used to represent w.

2.10 TYPE CASTS

Certain conversions are automatically performed by C. For example, if we divide an `int` by a `float`, the `int` is automatically converted to `float` before the division and the result is of type `float`. The type of an expression is explicitly changed by a *type cast operator*, which is simply any arithmetic or pointer type enclosed in parentheses. (Pointers are defined in Chapter 4.) For example, to find the greatest integer less than or equal to the square root of an integer i:

```
x = (int) sqrt((double)i);
```

EXERCISES

1. Write a program to compute the number of minutes, hours, and days in a given number of seconds.

2. What output should you expect from the following program?
   ```
   main()
   {
   int n = 69;
   printf("n = %d, n = %o, n = %x", n,n,n);
   }
   ```

3. Which of these are invalid variable names and why?

   ```
   FLOAT       1st

   _of_items   integer
   int         value_in_$
   N_3
   ```

4. What output should you expect from the following program?
   ```
   main()
   {
   int a = 35, b, c,d;
   b = a << 3;
   c = b | 7;
   d = 0 << 3 & c;
   printf("a = %d, b = %d, c = %d, d = %d\n",a,b,c,d);
   }
   ```

5. C Puzzles: inspired by [Feuer, 1982]

   What output should you expect from the following program?
   ```
   main()
   {
   int x,y,z;

   x = y = z = 1;
   printf("%d \n", -10 * x++ % 6 / 3); /* precedence*/
   x *= y + z; printf("%d\n",x);       /* *= operator*/
   printf("%d\n", x == ( y != z) );    /* relational
                                          operators*/
   printf("%d\n", ! y | y );           /* logical and bit
                                          operators*/
   ```

```
    printf("%d\n", x & y && z );        /* bit operator */
    y <<= 4;
    printf("%d\n",y);
    x = y = z = 1;    /*logical and increment operator*/
    --x || ++y && ++z;
    printf("%d, %d, %d\n",x,y,z);
    ++x || y++ && z++;
    printf("%d, %d, %d\n",x,y,z);
}
```

3
CONTROL STRUCTURES

In this chapter we will examine the way program flow is controlled in C. Simple decisionmaking is implemented through the `if` statement.

3.1 THE if STATEMENT

The *if statement* in C is similar to other programming languages. The format is the following:

```
if (expression)
  statement;
```

If the expression value is nonzero, then the statement is executed. A statement may be a simple statement or a compound statement called a block. In C a block is a group of statements within a pair of braces. A block may be used anywhere a simple statement is permitted.

3.2 THE if-else STATEMENT

The more general form of the `if` construct is the *if-else statement*. The format is the following:

```
if (expression)
  statement1;
else
  statement2;
```

If the value of the expression is nonzero, then statement1 is executed, otherwise statement2 is executed. In the `if-else` construct either statement1 or state-

```
if ( n % 2 == 0) /*if n is divisible by two*/
 {
 printf("The number is even.\n");
 printf("Half of the number is: %d\n",n/2);
 }
else
 printf("The number is odd.\n");
```

FIGURE 3.1 An illustration of the `if-else` construct

ment2 is always executed. Figure 3.1 is an example of how to determine if an int n is even or odd and compute half of n if it is even.

3.3 THE NESTED if

In the above example (Figure 3.1), we may wish to consider only positive integers. Figure 3.2 is a modification of the above example using nested if statements. Another way to accomplish the task shown in Figure 3.2 is shown in Figure 3.3.

```
if ( n > 0 )
 if ( n % 2 == 0 ) /*if n is divisible by 2*/
  {
  printf("The positive number is even.\n");
  printf("Half of the positive number is: %d\n",
         n/2);
  }
 else
  printf("The positive number is odd.\n");
else
 printf("The number is negative.\n");
```

FIGURE 3.2 An illustration of the `if-else` construct

```
if ( n > 0  && n % 2 == 0 )
 {
 printf("The positive number is even.\n");
 printf("Half the positive number is: %d",n/2);
 }
else if ( n > 0 )
 printf("The positive number is odd);
else
 printf("The number is negative.\n");
```

FIGURE 3.3 An illustration of the `else-if` construct

Normally the `else`-part in an `if-else` construct is indented so that it lines up with the if. It is, however, customary to use the indenting format of Figure 3.4 (next page) when there is a series of `else-if` statements.

3.4 THE switch STATEMENT

The *switch construct* in C allows one of several sections of code to be executed depending on the value of an integer expression. The usual format is the following:

```
switch ( expression )
 {
 case value1:
  statements_1;
  break;
 case value2:
  statements_2;
   break;

  . . .

 case valuen:
  statements_n;
  break;
 default:
  statements_d;
  break;
 }
```

The value in each case label is a constant. Control is transferred to the first statement following the case label whose value is the value of the expression. If none of the case label values equals the value of the expression, control is transferred to the statement following the label `default`, or, if no `default` label is present, to the statement after the switch statement. The *break statement* causes control to jump to the statement following the switch statement. Several case labels may appear in succession with no intervening statements.

The sequence of else-if statements shown in Figure 3.4 describes a grading scheme for a student's test score.

The program in Figure 3.5 (next page) implements this grading scheme using the switch construct.

The `break` statement in C also has a more general use. It can be used inside a loop to terminate a loop statement immediately and transfer control to the statement following the loop statement. We will see an example of this loop termination when the for loop is introduced.

```
if ( score >= 90 )
 grade = 'A';
else if ( grade >= 80)
 grade = 'B';
else if ( grade >= 70 )
 grade = 'C';
else of ( grade >= 60)
  grade = 'D';
else
 grade = 'F';
```

FIGURE 3.4 A grading scheme using `else-if`

Program 3.5

```
/*program that determines a student's grade according to
  his or her score on a test.*/
main()
{
 int score, n;
 char grade;

 printf("Enter your test score.\n");
 scanf("%d", &score);
 n = score / 10;  /* n is the number of 10's in score*/
 switch (n)
   {
   case 10:
   case 9: grade = 'A'; break;
   case 8: grade = 'B'; break;
   case 7: grade = 'C'; break;
   case 6: grade = 'D'; break;
   default: grade = 'F'; break;
   }
 printf( "Your grade is: %c\n", grade);
}
```

Program 3.5 Outputs

```
Enter your test score.
78
Your grade is: C

Enter your test score.
99
Your grade is: A

Enter your test score.
45
Your grade is: F
```

FIGURE 3.5 Program to illustrate the `switch` statement

3.5 THE CONDITIONAL EXPRESSION OPERATOR

The absolute value of a number n can be expressed as follows:

```
if ( n < 0 )
 abs_n = -n;
else
 abs_n = n;
```

We also have a *conditional expression operator* in C with the following format:

```
condition ? expression1 : expression2;
```

If value of the condition is TRUE (nonzero), then expression1 is evaluated to produce the result of the conditional expression. Otherwise expression2 is evaluated and its value is the result. The following expresses the absolute value using the conditional operator:

```
abs_n = ( n < 0 ) ? -n : n;
```

If n is negative, the value of abs_n is -n, otherwise abs_n is n. We may also use more than one condition. For example:

```
sign_n = ( n == 0 ) ? 0 : ( ( n > 0 ) ? 1 : -1);
```

If n is zero, sign_n will be zero; if n is positive, sign_n will be 1; otherwise (if n is negative), sign_n will be -1.

3.6 LOOPING

There are three *looping constructs* in C: the `for`, the `while`, and the `do` statements.

The for Loop

The `for` *statement* in C is more general than other languages such as Pascal. The format is the following:

```
for ( initialization; loop_condition; loop_expression)
 statement;
```

1. The initialization statement is executed, then:
2. The loop_condition is evaluated.

   If the loop_condition is zero, the loop is terminated; otherwise the body of the loop is executed.
3. The loop_expression is executed.
4. Return to step 2.

Program 3.6

```
main()
 /*Program to print out a five-row right triangle of stars.*/
 {
 int i, j;
 for ( i = 1; i <= 5; ++i)
  {
  for ( j = 1; j <= 5-i; ++j)
  printf(" ");
  for ( ; j <= 5; ++j)
  printf("*");
  printf("\n");         /* end line*/
  }
 }
```

Program 3.6 output

```
    *
   **
  ***
 ****
*****
```

FIGURE 3.6 An illustration of the nested `for` loop

For example, the following `for` loop calculates the sum of the first 100 natural numbers:

```
for ( n = 1, sum = 0; n <= 100; ++n)
  sum += n;
```

Initially n is set to 1 and sum is set to 0. The loop expression ++n causes n to be incremented by one at the end of each iteration. The loop terminates when n becomes 101. Note that the statement sum += n is equivalent to sum=sum+n.

Any or all of the three parts of the header of the `for` loop (the initialization, loop_condition and loop_expression) may be omitted. The two semicolons are, however, required. If the loop_condition is missing, it is assumed that it is nonzero and the loop is an infinite loop (in which case the body of the loop presumably contains a break statement). It is also possible to have multiple expressions and more complex conditions, as in the example below:

```
for ( i = 0, j = 20; i < 50 && j > 0; ++i, j -= 2 )
```

The program in Figure 3.6 uses the nested for loop to print a right triangle of stars. In the above Program 3.6 the body of the outside `for` loop is a compound statement and must be enclosed in braces.

The break Statement

The following piece of code illustrates the use of the break statement in a loop.

```
for (sum = 0, count = 0; count < 100 ; ++count)
 {
 printf("Enter a positive integer, zero to stop.\n");
 scanf("%d",&n);
 if (n == 0)
  break; /*Loop terminated when zero is entered.*/
 sum += n;
 }
```

This `for` loop will sum integers entered by the user and stops either when the user enters the flag zero or 100 integers have been entered. The variable count will contain the number of integers summed.

The continue Statement

The `continue` statement can be used in a loop to skip the remainder of the loop body for the current iteration. For example, the following segment of code reads a list of 10 numbers and sums the nonnegative ones.

```
for (i = 1; i <= 10; ++i )
 {
 scanf("%d", number);
 if ( number <= 0 ) /* if number is not positive
                       continue the loop*/
  continue;
 sum += number;
 }
```

which is equivalent to the following:

```
for (i = 1; i <=10; ++i)
 {
 scanf("%d", number);
 if (number > 0)
  sum += number;
 }
```

The while Loop

Another looping construct in C is the *while* loop. The format is the following:

```
while ( expression )
 statement;
```

The expression is evaluated. If the value is nonzero, the statement is executed. This action is repeated until the expression takes on a zero value, at which time the loop is terminated.

```
for (initial_condition; loop_condition; loop_expression)
 statement;
```

is equivalent to the following:

```
    initial_condition;
    while (loop_expression)
      {
      statement;
      loop_expression;
      }
```

Euclid's algorithm for finding the greatest common divisor (gcd) of two nonnegative integers m and n is as follows: if one of the integers is zero, say m, then the gcd is n. Otherwise, the gcd(m , n) = gcd(n MOD m , m). For example, gcd(6 , 15) = gcd(3 , 6) = gcd(0 , 3) = 3. The program in Figure 3.7 computes the gcd of two nonnegative integers using Euclid's algorithm.

Program 3.7
```
main()
 /* program to find the gcd of two nonnegative
    integers, using Euclid's algorithm.*/
{
 int m, n, temp;

 printf("Enter two nonnegative integers.\n");
 scanf("%d%d", &m, &n);
 while (m != 0)
   {
   temp = m;   /*Save m in a temporary location*/
   m = n % m;  /*compute n MOD m*/
   n = temp;
   }
 printf("The gcd of the two numbers is %d .\n", n);
}
```

Program 3.7 Outputs
```
Enter two nonnegative integers.
6 15
The gcd of the two numbers is 3 .

Enter two nonnegative integers.
578 340
The gcd of the two numbers is 34 .

Enter two nonnegative integers.
6453 7235
The gcd of the two numbers is 1 .
```

FIGURE 3.7 Program to calculate the gcd using the `while` loop

The do-while Loop

The `do-while` construct is intended for use in situations where the loop will be executed at least once. The loop condition is checked at the end of the `do-while` loop, unlike the `for` and the `while` loop, where it is checked at the beginning. The format is the following:

```
do
 statement;
 while ( expression );
```

The statement is executed. The expression is evaluated. If the expression has a nonzero value, the statement is executed again. This process is continued until the expression becomes zero, at which point the loop is terminated.

3.7 THE goto STATEMENT

The break and the continue statements can be used to exit a single loop. The *goto statement* is often used to exit a nested loop. The statement

```
goto label;
```

will cause program flow to branch to the statement:

```
label: statement;
```

A label must satisfy the same rules as an identifier and must be immediately followed by a colon. The label may appear anywhere in the function where the `goto` statement appears. It may appear before or after the `goto` statement. The following piece of code uses a `goto` statement to exit a nested loop when the value of `number` becomes zero.

```
while ( . . .)
 for ( . . .)
  {
  . . .
  if ( !number ) /*if number is zero*/
   goto last_data;
  }
. . .
last_data: printf("Zero indicates no more data.\n");
```

The goto statement is avoided by most programmers, since its excessive use causes programs to become unreadable. It violates the principle of structured programming, which is important in C.

EXERCISES

1. The following piece of code computes the larger of two numbers, m and n.
   ```
   if ( m >n )
    largest = m;
   else
    largest = n;
   ```
   Use the conditional operator to write a statement that is equivalent to the above piece of code.

2. Write a program that asks the user to enter three integers, p, q and r, at the terminal. Use the nested if construct to sort the three values into ascending order. Display the sorted values.

3. Write a program that asks the user to type one digit per line and display the digit in English. For example, if a 4 is typed, the word FOUR should be displayed. The program should terminate when the user types the digit 0.

4. Modify Program 3.6 to print out an equilateral triangle. Each side should have five stars.

5. Write a program to reverse the digits of a positive integer.

6. C Puzzles: inspired by [Feuer, 1982]

   What output should you expect from the following program?
   ```
   main()
   {
    int x = 1, y = 0, z;
    if( x  =  y < 1 )    z = 3;      /* if else construct*/
    else if( x != y++ ) z = 2;
    printf("%d ,%d, %d\n",x,y,z);
    x = y = 0;                       /* while construct*/
    while( x < 5 ) y += x++;
    printf("%d ,%d\n",x,y);
    for( y = 1; y < 5; y++)
      x = y;
    printf("%d ,%d\n ", x, y);
   }
   ```

4
POINTERS, ARRAYS AND STRUCTURES

The feature that most notably distinguishes C from other procedural languages is its use of *pointers*. Pointers provide flexibility in defining complex data structures and a mechanism for passing arguments to functions by reference. (We will discuss functions more fully in the next chapter.) Since the concepts of pointers and arrays are inseparable in C, an understanding of pointers is necessary before one can appreciate arrays.

4.1 POINTERS

The value of a pointer is simply a memory address. The data object stored at this address may be referenced indirectly by using the pointer. The general format for a pointer declaration is:

```
<type> *<name>;
```

The type specifies the type of data object that the pointer addresses. When a variable named nbr of type `int` is declared, the compiler allocates a certain amount of memory for this variable starting at, let us say, location 2000. The "Address of" operator `&` yields the address of any data object, so in this case `&nbr` is 2000. The address of an integer variable is stored in a "pointer to int" and is, for example, declared by:

```
int *nbr_ptr;
```

The compiler will allocate for nbr_ptr the amount of memory required to store the address of an integer variable. The following assignment stores the address of nbr in the pointer nbr_ptr:

```
nbr_ptr = &nbr;
```

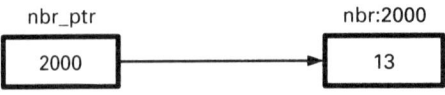

FIGURE 4.1 nbr_ptr pointing to nbr

Now the value of nbr_ptr is 2000. The assignment in Figure 4.1 stores the value 13 in the variable nbr:

```
*nbr_ptr = 13;
```

or equivalently:

```
nbr = 13;
```

Pointers allow us to change the value of a variable indirectly as illustrated in Figure 4.2.

The general format for an *array* is the following:

```
<type> <name>[count];
```

The entire array is referred to by name, which can be any legal variable name. The array holds count data objects of type `type`. For example, the following is a declaration of an array of size 50 of type int.

```
int scores[50];
```

The compiler will allocate enough storage for 50 values of type int for the array scores. The first element of the array is scores[0], and the last is scores[49]. In many contexts, the array name itself is actually a pointer to the first element of the array. So scores and &scores[0] both refer to the same address, and *scores is the same as scores[0]. To store the value 87 in scores[0], we could use

```
*scores = 87;
```

Other elements of the array are referenced by, for example, scores[5], or via a pointer. For example, to add the entries in scores, either of the following segments may be used:

```
int i;
long sum;
...
for (i = 49, sum = 0; i >= 0; --i)
  sum += scores[i];
```

or

```
    int *p;
    long sum;
    ...
    for (p = &scores[49]; p >= scores; --p)
     sum += *p;
```

Program 4.1
```
main()
 {
 int i1 = 10, i2;
 int *iptr1, *iptr2;
 int **iptr_ptr;   /* A pointer to a pointer to an int */
 char c = 'A';
 char *cptr = &c;
 float f = 2.5;
 float *fptr = &f;
 double d, *dptr = &d;

 iptr1 = &i1; /* iptr1 is the address of i1*/
 iptr2 = &i2; /* iptr2 is the address of i2*/
 *iptr2 = *iptr1 - 2;    /* same effect as i2 = i1 - 2 */
 iptr1 = iptr2; /* two pointers to the same integer */
 printf("i1 = %d, *iptr1 = %d\n",i1,*iptr1);
 printf("i2 = %d, *iptr2 = %d\n",i2,*iptr2);
 iptr_ptr = &iptr2;
 **iptr_ptr = 17;
 printf("After **iptr_ptr = 17:\n");
 printf("i2 = %d, iptr2 = %p\n", i2, iptr2);
 printf("iptr_ptr = %p, *iptr_ptr = %p, **iptr_ptr = %d\n",
        iptr_ptr, *iptr_ptr, **iptr_ptr);
 printf("c = %c, *cptr = %c\n",c,*cptr);
 printf("address of c : %p\n",cptr);
 *dptr = 15e12;
 printf("*dptr = %f\n",*dptr);
 printf("f = %f, *fptr = %f\n",f,*fptr);
 }
```

Program 4.1 output
```
i1 = 10, *iptr1 = 8
i2 = 8, *iptr2 = 8
After **iptr_ptr = 17:
i2 = 17, iptr2 = FFD6
iptr_ptr = FFD8, *iptr_ptr = FFD6, **iptr_ptr = 17
c = A, *cptr = A
address of c : FFDB
*dptr = 15000000000000.000000
f = 2.500000, *fptr = 2.500000
```

FIGURE 4.2 An illustration of pointer arithmetic

4.2 INITIALIZING ARRAYS

To initialize an array (at the start of program execution), the array declaration is followed by a list of values inside braces, as in:

```
static int scores[50] = {87,76};
```

The first two elements, scores[0] and scores[1], are initialized to the given values, and the remainder, scores[2], ..., scores[49], are initialized to zero. The presence of the "storage class" `static` will be explained in the next chapter. If all elements of the array are initialized, it is admissible to leave out the size. For example,

```
static int days[] = {31,28,31,30,31,30,31,31,30,31,30,31};
```

4.3 CHARACTER STRINGS

A *character string* is simply an array of type `char`. Strings in C are terminated by the null character '\0'. We can initialize character strings as follows:

```
char word[15] = {"First"};
```

which is equivalent to

```
char word[15] = {'F','i','r','s','t','\0'};
```

The compiler will allocate space for a 15-character array called "word." If we had omitted the size, the space allocation would have been for a character array of size six. The terminating null character '\0' is automatically inserted to indicate the end of the string. Strings are output using the format %s. The program in Figure 4.3 illustrates character arrays.

We start by initializing sentence as the empty character string and then concatenating input words to sentence until the first character of the input word is a period, at which point we output the sentence. The function `strcat` is one of several library functions available for use with strings. For a list of these functions, see Appendix C. Note that we do not need the address operator & when the string format %s is used in `scanf`, since the array name word is itself an address.

4.4 ENUMERATED TYPES

For variables with limited range, we can use the enumerated type. The general format for the enumerated type is:

```
enum <name>{value 1,value 2, . . .} variable list;
```

Program 4.2

```
/* Program to prompt the user for words and place
   them in a sentence.  The end of the sentence is indicated
   by an input beginning with the character ".".
   The sentence is then output */

main()
 {
 char word[15];
 char sentence[150] = "\0"; /*Initially, the empty string*/

 do
  {
  printf("Enter a word, period ends sentence.\n");
  scanf("%s", word);
  strcat(sentence,word);
  strcat(sentence, " ");
  }
  while ( word[0] != '.');
 printf("The sentence you input is:\n%s\n",sentence);
 }
```

Program 4.2 output

```
Enter a word, period ends sentence.
Strings
Enter a word, period ends sentence.
are
Enter a word, period ends sentence.
fun
Enter a word, period ends sentence.
.
The sentence you input is:
Strings are fun .
```

FIGURE 4.3 Program to illustrate character strings

For example, the days of the week can be defined as:

```
enum days { Monday, Tuesday, Wednesday,
            Thursday, Friday} a_day;
```

The variable a_day is of type enum days, and we can assign values to it as follows:

```
a_day = Tuesday;
++a_day;
```

Now a_day will be associated with the enumeration identifier Wednesday. The compiler assigns a sequence of integers starting with 0 to the enumeration identifiers. We may assign our own values, such as:

```
enum coins { dollars = 100, quarters = 25, dimes = 10,
             nickels = 5, pennies = 1 };
```

4.5 STRUCTURES

Structures are C's data type for dealing with data that is composed of values of different types. Structures are equivalent to records in Pascal. The general format for a structure is the following:

```
struct name
 {
 field declaration;
 field declaration;
 ...
 } variable list;
```

The name of the structure is optional. For example, to store information about students, we may want to have for each name, the number of credits earned so far, grade point average field and the gender field:

```
struct student
 {
 char name[15];
 int  credits;
 float GPA;
 char gender;
 } a_student;
```

The variable a_student is of type `struct` student. Now that this type is defined, we may define:

```
struct student another_student;
```

We can assign values to the fields by using the select member operator ".".

```
strcpy (a_student.name , "Mary-Jones");
a_student.credits = 58;
a_student.GPA = 2.9;
a_student.gender = 'f';
```

Note that we must use the library string copy function `strcpy` in order to assign a value to the name field. Structures can be initialized as follows:

```
static struct student person =
 {
 "Harry Smith",
 46,
 2.6,
 'm'
 };
```

We can define an array of structures as follows:

```
struct student students[30];
```
To assign credits to the first element of the array:
```
students[0].credits = 79;
```
If student_ptr is defined by
```
struct student *student_ptr;
```
then the credits field is referenced by
```
student_ptr->credits
```
which is an abbreviated form of
```
(*student_ptr).credits
```
The program in Figure 4.4 (next page) inputs student records and outputs them to the screen.

4.6 UNIONS

Unions are like structures in that they can have fields of varying types. The storage allocation for unions is, however, different from structures. The compiler will allocate enough storage for the largest field of the union. The union may contain a value for only one field at a time. This construct is similar to Pascal's variant record. The general format for a union is as follows:
```
union <name>
 {
 field declaration;
 field declaration;
 ...
 } variable list;
```
The name is optional. For example, a variable of the following union type may contain an `int` or a `float`.
```
union number
 {
 int i;
 float f;
 } ;
```
We can have arrays or structures containing unions, such as:
```
struct
 {
 char name[8];
 union number n;
 } value;
```

Program 4.3
```
#define MAX_STUDENTS 30 /* A name for the constant */
main()
/* This program will ask as input the college GPA and
   student records, and will output them.*/
{
int j,i = 0;
struct student
 {
 char name[15]; /*There are at most 15 characters in a name*/
 int credits;
 float GPA;
 char gender;
 };
struct student class[MAX_STUDENTS]; /*class is an array of students*/
float college_GPA;

printf("Enter the college GPA.\n");
scanf("%f",&college_GPA);
for (i = 0; i < MAX_STUDENTS; ++i)
 {
 printf("Enter a student name, Z to terminate.\n");
 scanf("%15s", class[i].name);
 if (class[i].name[0] == 'Z' ||
     class[i].name[0] == 'z')
  break;
 printf("Enter student's credits GPA and sex.\n");
 scanf("%d%f %c",&class[i].credits,&class[i].GPA, &class[i].gender);
 /* The format "%d%f %c" scans for an integer a floating point number and skips
    whitespace until a character is encountered.*/
 printf("Enter another student name\n");
 }
```

FIGURE 4.4 (continues next page)

The following code segment will examine the name field of value and print out a_number with the correct format:

```
        if (strcmp(value.name,"integer") == 0)
         printf("value = %d\n",value.n.i);
        else if (strcmp(value.name,"floating") == 0)
         printf("value = %f\n",value.n.f);
```

```
    printf("The college grade point average is: %5.2f\n", college_GPA);
    printf("     name          credits    GPA   sex\n");
    for( j = 0; j < i; ++j)
     {
     printf("%-15s    %3d   ", class[j].name,class[j].credits);
     printf("%5.2f    %c\n",class[j].GPA,class[j].gender);
     }
    }
```

Program 4.3 output

```
Enter the college GPA.
2.3
Enter a student name, Z to terminate.
Mary-Jones
Enter student's credits GPA and sex.
56 3.4 f
Enter another student name
Enter a student name, Z to terminate.
Bill-Smith
Enter student's credits GPA and sex.
34 2.3 m
Enter another student name
Enter a student name, Z to terminate.
z
The college grade point average is:  2.30
     name          credits    GPA   sex
Mary-Jones            56      3.40   f
Bill-Smith            34      2.30   m
```

FIGURE 4.4 Program to illustrate records

4.7 SIZEOF OPERATOR

One operator we did not mention in Chapter 2 is the *sizeof operator*, which yields the number of bytes of storage required by its operand. The operand is either a data type or a variable name. For example, if nbr is of type union number (as defined above), then sizeof(nbr) = sizeof(union number) = sizeof(float) (which is typically 4). Given the declarations

```
    char chrs[30];
    char chr_ptr = chrs;
```

then sizeof(chrs) is 30; sizeof(chr_ptr) is the number of bytes in a pointer to **char**; and sizeof(*chr_ptr) = sizeof(chrs[0]) = sizeof(char) = 1. Note that sizeof(*chr_ptr) is neither the size of the array chrs nor the length of the string stored there.

4.8 MULTIDIMENSIONAL ARRAYS

Two-dimensional arrays in C are declared as follows:

```
<type> <name> [row size][column size];
```

For example, the following is a 2 x 4 matrix of real numbers.

```
float matrix[2][4] = { {2.5,  2  , -3.67,  0},
                       {3  , 2.7,  5.8 , -3}}
```

The value of matrix[0][2] is -3.67, since arrays always begin with index zero in C. Note that matrix[i], i = 0,1, is an array of length four of type `float`. In particular, `sizeof(maxtrix[1])` is `4*sizeof(float)`.

In the above example the inner braces are optional. If, however, only parts of the array are initialized, then they are required, as in the following example.

```
int m[4][6] = { { 3,  6,  8    }
                { 0, -1, 66 ,4 }
                {              }
                { 1,  2,       }
              }
```

The indicated elements will be initialized and the remaining elements will be set to zero. For example, m[3][0] will have the value 1 and m[2][1], the value 0.

EXERCISES

1. Write a program to reverse the entries of a 5-floating-point array. Write a second version of the above program using pointers only.
2. Using pointers, write a program that will compare two input strings and determine if they are identical. This program should perform the same purpose as the library function `strcmp`.
3. Using enumerated types, write a program that will determine if tomorrow will be a weekend or a weekday, given the day of the week today.
4. Define a structure called time with hour, minute and seconds fields. Write a program that will accept as input a certain time and will compute what time it will be after a specified input length of time has passed. For example, if 10:15:50 is input after a length of time 4:5:32, the program should compute the time to be 2:21:22.
5. Write a program that will read in the average college GPA and data for a given number of students of the above type "student," and compute the total number of credits they have earned and the average of their GPA.
6. C Puzzles: inspired by [Feuer, 1982]

    What output should you expect from the following program?

4.8 MULTIDIMENSIONAL ARRAYS

```
main()
{
 int a[] = {1,2,3,4,5};
 int i, *p;
 int *pp[5]; /* array of pointers*/
 int **qq = pp;
 for ( p = &a[0], i = 1; i < 5; i++ ) /*pointers & arrays*/
  printf( "%d", p[i] );
 printf("\n");
 *pp = a;
 printf("%d ,%d ,%d\n",*p, *pp[0], **qq);
 qq++;
 printf("%d\n", qq-pp);
 *p++;
 printf("%d ,%d\n",*p,**--qq);
}
```

5
FUNCTIONS

Every C program consists of one or more functions. The program examples so far have consisted of the function `main`. (Indeed, every C program must include a function called `main`.) We have also used library functions such as `printf`, `scanf`, `strcpy`, etc. Functions are the building blocks of programming in C. The correct use of functions will produce efficient and comprehensible programs that are easy to maintain and modify.

5.1 FUNCTION FORMAT

The general format for a *function* definition is:

```
<type> <name> (<parameter list>)
 {
 declarations
 statements
 return <value>
 }
```

We will discuss this syntax subsequently. For now let us look at an example. The following function returns the average of an array of floating-point numbers:

```
float average(float x[], int n)
/* compute the average of x[0], ..., x[n-1] */
{
 int i;
 double sum = 0;

 if (x == NULL || n <= 0)
  return 0.0;
 for (i = 0; i < n; ++i)
  sum += x[i];
 return sum / n;
}
```

The function might be invoked as follows:

```
float avg_score;
float scores[4];
/* read in the scores */
 . . .
avg_score = average(scores, 4);
```

5.2 PARAMETER LIST

The parameter list consists of ordinary variable declarations separated by commas. In C function arguments are passed by value. This means, in essence, that the parameters of a function are local variables. When the function is invoked, the parameters are initialized by the value of the actual arguments. Thus a function that swaps two integer variables must be written:

```
void swap(int *n1_ptr, int *n2_ptr)
{
 int temp = *n1_ptr;
 *n1_ptr = *n2_ptr;
 *n2_ptr = temp;
 return;
}
```

The call for swapping the variables *i* and *j* would be:

```
swap(&i, &j);
```

When the function is invoked, n1_ptr and n2_ptr are initialized with the addresses of *i* and *j* respectively.

The parameters may be of any data type. For example, the parameter could be a structure. Since the parameter is a local copy of the actual argument, a structure argument must be copied when the function is invoked, which can be a time-consuming operation for large structures. In such cases, the parameter is usually a pointer to a structure instead of the structure itself.

There is one limitation: unlike a structure, an array in its entirety cannot be passed to a function. Of course, the address of an array may be passed to a function as in the function average above. When the name of an array is used as an argument in a function call, the compiler converts the argument to a pointer to the first element of the array.

5.3 RETURN TYPE

A function can return any valid type except a function or an array. (The *return type* can be a pointer to a function or array.) The value of the expression in the return statement must be compatible with the declared type of the function. If the function does not return a value, the return type should be `void`.

5.4 FUNCTION PROTOTYPES

Notice that in the function average above, the compiler must know that the return type of the function is `float`. This can be accomplished in two ways. The function definition itself may appear in the source file before it is referenced. A more flexible mechanism is provided by function prototypes.

A *function prototype* is (in its simplest form) just the opening part of a function definition. A common programming practice is to include at the beginning of each source file a function prototype for each function defined in that file. (Prototypes for functions defined in other modules are usually listed in "header files." See Chapter 8.) Here are three examples:

```
float average(float x[], int n);
int gcd(int n, int m);
int get_videotype(void);
```

The second prototype declares a function that accepts two integer arguments and returns an integer. (Note that the type `int` must be repeated in the parameter list.) The third function, get_videotype, takes no arguments, which is indicated by the parameter list `void`. (For historical reasons, the absence of parameters cannot be indicated in a function prototype by an empty parameter list.)

Since function prototypes also specify the parameter types, the compiler can (and does) check that each argument appearing in a function call is of the correct type. If the types do not match, the compiler converts the argument to the correct type, if possible. Otherwise the compiler signals an error.

5.5 FUNCTION BODY

The *function body* immediately follows the parameter list. The body consists of a compound statement called a block. A block begins with variable declarations, followed by one or more statements. The entire block is delimited by braces.

(Note that a block may appear anywhere a statement is required. Also note that nested function definitions are not allowed.)

5.6 STORAGE CLASSES

The scope or visibility of a variable is determined by the placement of its declaration and by storage class modifiers.

Static and Auto Variables

Variables defined inside a function are local to that function and cannot be accessed by other functions. The variables *i* and *sum* in the function average above have the default storage class `auto`. This means that the variable is created whenever the function is entered and discarded when the function is exited. If we wish to maintain the value of a local variable in successive function calls, we must use the storage class `static`. For example:

```
int read_data(char *buffer)
{
 static int first_call = 1;
 . . .
 if (first_call)
 {
  first_call = 0;
  /* Open data file */
  . . .
 }
 . . .
}
```

An array (or structure) that is defined and initialized inside a function, as illustrated in the previous chapter, should normally have `static` storage class. (Otherwise the array must be initialized every time the function is invoked.)

Figure 5.1 illustrates `static` and `auto` variables.

Global Variables

Variables that are declared outside of any function are *global variables* and are accessible from any function following the declaration. In addition a global variable is accessible from other source files unless the storage class `static` is specified. (In this context `static` has a different meaning than described above.) This applies to functions as well: a function definition that begins with the storage class keyword `static` may be accessed only by functions defined in the same source file.

Program 5.1
```
void local(void);
main()
{
 local();
 local();
}

void local()
{
 int auto auto_var = 2;
 int static static_var = 2;

 auto_var--;
 static_var--;
 printf("auto_var = %d, static_var = %d\n",
   auto_var,static_var);
}
```

Program 5.1 output
```
auto_var = 1, static_var = 1
auto_var = 1, static_var = 0
```

FIGURE 5.1 Program to illustrate `static` and `auto` variables

To access a variable defined in a separate source file, we use the storage class `extern`. For example:

```
extern int errorlevel;
```

specifies that errorlevel is an integer variable defined in another source file.

The declaration of global variables is desirable when many functions must reference the same variable. Figure 5.2 (see next page) illustrates the use of global variables.

The variables, numbers, and n are defined outside the functions and can be referenced by all the functions in this file.

5.7 SEPARATE COMPILATIONS AND EXTERNAL VARIABLES AND FUNCTIONS

We have so far limited our programs to single files. This is not practical when dealing with large programs. C provides the facility to write functions in several files and compile them separately. Usually functions are grouped in separate files called modules according to the way in which they logically fit together. There must be exactly one file that contains the function "main." As mentioned above, prototypes for each nonstatic function are collected in one or

Program 5.2

```
/* program to compute minimum of an array of numbers, sort
   it, and print it.*/

int numbers[] = {3,5,-4,7,0,-5,1,6,34,5};
int n = 10;

int min(void);
void sort(void);
void swap(int *a_pointer, int *b_pointer);
void print_nums(void);

main()
{
 print_nums();
 printf("\nThe smallest number is = %d\n",min());
 sort();
 printf("After sorting, ");
 print_nums();

}
int min()
{
 int i,smallest;

 smallest = numbers[0];
 for ( i = 1; i < n; i++)
 if(numbers[i] < smallest)
  smallest = numbers[i];
 return(smallest);
}
void sort()
/* a simple bubble sort sorting in ascending order*/
{
 int i,j;
 for ( i = 0; i < n-1; i++)
  for (j = i + 1; j < n; j++)
   if(numbers[i] > numbers[j])
    swap(&numbers[i], &numbers[j]);
}
```

FIGURE 5.2 (continues next page)

more header files. These header files are combined with each source file at compilation time. The details of how this is accomplished are in Chapter 8.

We need to compile each module only once. When we are ready to run the program, the separate object modules will be linked together and an executable file created.

In Turbo C a project file is created with the names of all the modules. The ProjectMake facility then creates the executable file to be run. See Chapter 9.

```
void swap(int *a_pointer, int *b_pointer)
/* function to interchange a and b*/
{
 int temp;

 temp = *a_pointer;
 *a_pointer = *b_pointer;
 *b_pointer = temp;
}
void print_nums()
/*function to print a global array of integers*/
{
 int i;
 printf("The numbers are:\n");
 for ( i = 0; i < n; i++)
  printf("%5d",numbers[i]);
}
```

Program 5.2 output

```
The numbers are:
    3    5   -4    7    0   -5    1    6   34    5
The smallest number is = -5
After sorting, The numbers are:
   -5   -4    0    1    3    5    5    6    7   34
```

FIGURE 5.2 An illustration of global variable and pointer argument

5.8 RECURSION

The factorial function n! is a common example of a recursive function defined in terms of itself:

```
0! = 1
n! = n x (n-1)!
```

The C language supports *recursion*. Although recursive functions are not always the most economic way of performing a task, their simplicity more than compensates for their possible inefficiency.

Factorial function

```
long fact(int n);
{
 long temp;

 if( n === 0 )
  temp = 1;
 else
  temp = n * fact(n-1);
 return temp;
}
```

Call to fact

```
long i;
...
i = fact(8);
```

Note that the above function is equivalent to:

```
long fact(int n)
{
   return (n <= 0) ? 1 : n * fact(n-1);
}
```

EXERCISES

1. Write a function that computes an integral power of an integer value. The function power should have two `int` arguments and return a `long int`.
2. Write two versions of a function that adds two 3 x 4 matrices. The first version should have three arguments: two for the given matrices and one for the result matrix. The second version should have two arguments and place the result in a globally defined matrix.
3. Write a function to test if a string of characters is a palindrome. A palindrome is a character string that is the same read forward or backward, such as sees or mom. Include a function to reverse a character string.
4. Write a function that will count the number of words in a character string. The only argument this function should have is a pointer to the character string. Words are separated by blanks.
5. Change the sort function of program 5.4 to sort in descending instead of ascending order.
6. C Puzzle: inspired by [Feuer, 1982]

    What output should you expect from the following program?

    ```
    int i = 0;
    main()
    {
     auto int i = 1;
     printf("%d\n", i);
     {
      int i = 2;
      printf("%d\n", i);
      i +=2;
      printf("%d\n", i);
     }
     printf("%d\n", i);
    }
    ```

6
INPUT AND OUTPUT

6.1 STANDARD I/O

We have so far used several functions such as `printf`, `scanf`, and `getchar` to input and output data from and to the computer screen. Although these library functions are not a part of the core language, their behavior is part of the definition of the C language. The *standard header* file named "stdio.h" contains function prototypes for each of the input/output functions. (Various constants are also defined in `stdio.h`.) The directive

    #include <stdio.h>

causes the body of `stdio.h` to be processed by the compiler as part of the program text. (More on the `include` directive in Chapter 8.)

The i/o functions in C deal with *streams*. A stream is just a sequence of bytes that is read or, in the case of output, generated by a program. The source or destination of the stream might be an ordinary data file stored on a disk or an interactive device such as the keyboard. How to connect a stream to a file will be discussed later in this chapter. Once the connection is established, references to the stream are made through a "file pointer."

Three special streams are automatically opened when the program begins execution. Their file pointers (defined in stdio.h) are `stdin` (standard input, usually the keyboard), `stdout` (standard output, usually the screen), and `stderr` (error output). Some functions, such as `printf` and `scanf`, use these streams implicitly.

    int printf(const char *format, <argument list>);

The function `printf` formats output and writes it to `stdout`. Each argument in the argument list is converted to an external representation under the control of a conversion specifier (signaled by the percent sign `%`) in the character string "`format`." Text in the format string other than conversion specifiers is output unaltered. (Escape sequences such as \t are replaced by their external representations.)

43

TABLE 6.1 Conversion specifics for the `printf` function (continued next page)

flag
- `-`   Left justify.
- `+`   Print with sign, + or -.
- blank   Nonnegative numbers preceded by a blank.
- `#`   Octal number prefixed by 0; hex number prefixed by 0x or 0X; decimal points always appear in e, E, f, g, G format; trailing zeros appear in g, G format.
- `0`   Leading zeros instead of blanks.

width   Minimum number of character positions.

precision   Minimum number of digits for integer conversions; maximum number of characters for a string; maximum number of digits after the decimal point for the floating conversions e, E and f; maximum number of significant digits for G and g.

size   Override default size of argument.
- h   for `short`.
- l   for `long`.
- L   for `long double`.

type
- integer
  - d   `signed int`.
  - u   `unsigned int`.
  - o   `unsigned` octal.
  - x   `unsigned` hexadecimal with (a,b,c,d,e,f).
  - X   `unsigned` hexadecimal with (A,B,C,D,E,F).
- floating point
  - f   Signed value of the form [-]dd.dd.
  - e   Signed value of the form [-]d.dde[+/-]dd.
  - E   Signed value of the form [-]d.ddE[+/-]dd.
  - g   f or e format is used, whichever takes less space without sacrificing precision.
  - G   Same as g except E instead of e is used.
- character
  - c   Single character.
  - s   String terminated by a null character.
  - %   Percent sign.
- pointer
  - p   Pointer.

An output conversion specifier has the form

```
% <flag> <width> . <precision> <size> <type>
```

Only the <type> is required. (If the <precision> is omitted, then the preceding decimal point is also omitted.)

The flag is one of the following shown in Table 6.1.

Program 2.1 Some features of the `printf` function

```
int scanf(const char *format, <address list> );
```

The **scanf** function reads characters from `stdin` (standard input) and converts them to internal form under control of the format string `format`. Conversions are specified in a manner similar to those for the `printf` function:

```
% <width> <size> <type>
```

Table 6.2 shows the possible conversions. If the conversion type is "c," then the next input character is stored, even if it is a whitespace character (space, tab, form feed or newline). If the width w is greater than 1, then the next w characters are stored in the character array named in the corresponding argument in the call to `scanf`.

For strings (conversion type "s"), any initial whitespace characters are skipped; the sequence of characters stored starts with the first nonwhitespace character and is terminated by the next whitespace character. As usual, the null character is stored after the last stored character. Thus the argument must point to a character array long enough to contain the longest possible string that might appear in the input plus one for the null character.

If the conversion type is "n," then the number of characters read so far is stored.

If an asterisk (*) immediately follows the percent sign, then the next input item is skipped.

Any literal text in the format string must match the next characters from the input. For example, the `scanf` call

```
scanf("%s /%d %c%s,%d:%d",wk_day,&day,&ch,month,&hr,&min);
```

with the line of input

```
Monday / 22 / October, 10:19:40
```

would store the string Monday in wk_day, and 22 in day, October in month, 10 in hr, and 19 in min. If no space were placed between %d and %c, then the space would be read into ch and / into month. The space after %d caused the whitespace to be skipped before the character assignment was made to ch.

If the `scanf` function encounters unexpected characters it will terminate its scan and return the number of items successfully read. The call to `scanf`

```
scanf("%d %d %s",&i1,&i2,string1);
```

will return the value 1 if the following line of input is typed:

TABLE 6.2 Conversion specifiers for the `scanf` function

width: Maximum number of positions a field occupies.
  size
      h   `short int`.
      l   `long` for integer type and double for float type.
      L   `long double` (float type only).
  type

Character	Expected input	Argument is pointer to
integer		
d[D]	Decimal integer	`int [long]`
o [O]	Octal integer	`int [long]`
i[I]	Decimal, octal or hexadecimal	`int [long]`
u[U]	unsigned decimal integer	`unsigned int [singed long]`
x[X]	hexadecimal int	`int [long]`
floating point		
f, e, E, g, G	Floating point	`float`
character		
c	Character	`char`
s	Character string	array of `char`
%	The % character	
pointer		
p	Hexadecimel	Pointer to an object
n		int

```
34 hello
```

The call will store 34 in i1 and will encounter the character "h" when it is expecting an integer. The scan is terminated.

Four other standard I/O functions use `stdin` and `stdout` but without formatting:

```
int getchar(void);
int putchar(int c);
char *gets(char *buffer);
int *puts(char *buffer);
```

The function `getchar` returns the next character from the stream `stdin` or, if `stdin` is at the end of file, the constant `EOF` (defined in stdio.h). The function `putchar` writes one character to `stdout`.

Entire lines may be transferred using `gets` and `puts`. The function `gets` reads characters from `stdin` until the newline character is encountered. These characters are stored in the string buffer with a null character appended to the end. The newline character is not stored. Notice that buffer must be large enough to hold the longest line that might be input. If the stream `stdin` is at the end of file, `gets` returns the null pointer. (Otherwise it returns buffer.)

The function `puts` writes the string buffer to the stream `stdout` and appends a newline character.

6.2 EXTERNAL FILES

It is often more convenient to use files other than `stdin` and `stdout` to input and output data. On computers running DOS or UNIX™, one way to do this is to specify the input and the output files as part of the command line. If prog1.exe is a successfully compiled and linked executable file, the command

```
prog1 < prog1.in > prog1.out
```

will execute the program prog1 and "redirect" `stdin` to the file prog1.in and redirect all output from stdout to the file prog1.out. All calls to `printf` and `scanf` will be automatically redirected to these files.

A program may access a file directly by connecting a stream to it. A stream is connected to a file or device by calling `fopen`. The function `fopen` returns a pointer to an object of type FILE. This "file pointer" is used for all subsequent I/O operations. A prototype for `fopen` is the following:

```
FILE *fopen(char *filename, char *mode);
```

The type `FILE` is defined in the header file stdio.h. It is normally a structure containing the information required by the various I/O functions.

The first argument is a name of a file or device. (What constitutes a valid name depends on the operating system being used.) The second argument indicates the kind of I/O operation we intend to perform on this file: "r" for read, "w" for write, and "a" for append.

The program in Figure 6.1 will copy the content of prog1.in to prog1.out. We will use command line arguments. This is done by including two parameters in the function main:

```
main(int argc, char *argv[])
```

`argc` refers to the number of parameters in the command line and `argv[i]` is a string containing the i-th command line argument. `argv[0]` will contain the name of the program, so `argc` is at least one.

Program 6.1
```
/* program to copy the file named in the first command
 *line argument to the file named in the second command
 * line argument.*/
#include <stdio.h>
#include <stdlib.h>   /* Definition of EXIT_FAILURE */
main(int argc,char *argv[])
{
 FILE *in,*out;
 int ch;
 int i;
 for(i = 1; i < argc ; i++)
  {
  /* echo command line arguments*/
  printf("argv[%-d] = %s\n",i,argv[i]);
  }
 if (argc != 3)
  {
  fprintf(stderr, "Usage: copy_file old_file new_file\n");
  exit(EXIT_FAILURE);   /* Quit with error */
  }
 in = fopen(argv[1],"r"); /*file to copy from*/
 out = fopen(argv[2],"w"); /* file to copy to*/
 while( (ch = getc(in)) != EOF )
  putc(ch, out);
 fclose(argv[1]);
 fclose(argv[2]);
 return EXIT_SUCCESS;
}
```

Program input (in_file):
```
File to be
copied.
```

Command line:
```
copy_file in_file out_file
```

Program output:
```
argv[1] = in_file
argv[2] = out_file
file in_file was copied to file out_file.
```

FIGURE 6.1 Illustration of command line arguments and external files

We have used three new functions in program 6.1: `getc`, `putc` and `fclose`. The functions `getc` and `putc` are similar to the functions `getchar` and `putchar` with the difference that `getc` and `putc` require a file pointer argument that determines which stream to read from or write to.

The function `fclose` "closes" a file when it is no longer needed. If there is an error in closing the file, `fclose` returns the value `EOF`. Since most systems do not allow more than a certain number of files to be open at the same time, it is good practice to close a file when not in use.

fprintf and fscanf

The functions `fprintf` and `fscanf` are the external file versions of `printf` and `scanf`. They have an additional first argument, a file pointer, that determines which stream to write to or read from. The statement

```
fprintf(stdout, "Files are fun.\n");
```

is equivalent to

```
printf("Files are fun.\n");
```

fgets and fputs

These functions, like `gets` and `puts`, are used to read and write lines of text. Beside taking a file pointer as an argument, they differ from `gets` and `puts` in their treatment of the newline character. The prototype for `fgets` is the following:

```
char *fgets(char *buffer, int n, FILE *fp);
```

This function reads characters into buffer from the stream `fp` until a newline character is stored in buffer or n-1 characters are read. If the stream `fp` is at the end of file when `fgets` is called, then `fgets` returns NULL; otherwise it returns buffer. The string in buffer is always terminated by the null character (unless `fgets` returns NULL).

The prototype for `fputs` is the following:

```
int fputs(char *buffer, FILE *fp);
```

The string buffer is written to the stream `fp`. If an error occurs, `fputs` returns EOF.

6.3 RANDOM ACCESS

We often want to access files in ways other than sequentially. To do this the functions `fseek` and `ftell` are used. The function prototype for `fseek` is the following:

```
fseek(FILE *fp, long offset, int specifier);
```

The function `fseek` is called to move to a particular position in a file. The argument offset determines the number of bytes to move from either the beginning of the file (specifier = 0), the current position (specifier = 1), or the end of the file (specifier = 2), as illustrated in the following calls:

```
fseek(fp,n,0);   /*go to the nth byte in the file*/
fseek(fp,n,2);   /*go to n bytes before the end of file*/
fseek(fp,-n,1);  /*go back n bytes*/
```

To identify the current byte location in a file we use the `ftell` function, which takes a file pointer as an argument and returns a `long int`, the position of the next byte to be read or written to.

6.4 BINARY I/O

It is possible to read and write data other than character type to files in C. We must, however, use the functions `fread` and `fwrite`. The prototype for `fread` is:

```
unsigned fread(void *ptr, unsigned size, unsigned n, FILE *fp);
```

The companion function `fwrite` has the same prototype. For example, the following `fwrite` call writes 10 student records to the file pointed to by fp;

```
struct student students[10];
...
fwrite(students, sizeof(struct student), 10, fp);
```

This single `fwrite` call writes 10 records at once to a file.

EXERCISES

1. Using `getc`, write a function to return the number of characters in an external file.
2. Using `fscan`, write a function to return the number of words in an external file.
3. Using `fgets`, write a function to return the number of lines in an external file.
4. Write a program that uses arguments on the command line to perform the task of counting the number of characters, words, or lines in a file. Use the functions written for the above three exercises.

7
DYNAMIC DATA STRUCTURES

The data structures we have considered so far all have one property in common: The compiler knows their sizes and ensures that the proper storage will be allocated for them. It is not always possible to know how much storage is needed for the data at the time the source program is being created. This problem is solved by the use of *dynamic data structures* like linked lists. Dynamic data structures are designed to allow the size of the data to grow at the time the program is being executed. A second feature of dynamic data structures is very useful. In array structures, in order to insert or delete data we need to shift the elements of array to make room or to close up gaps. This problem does not exist in dynamic data structures, since we need only to move pointers in order to delete or insert.

7.1 typedef

In C it is possible to define synonyms for data types. `typedef` can appear outside functions and is like a variable declaration in syntax. For example:

```
typedef int integer;
typedef float real;
typedef char string[100];
typedef char *char_pointer;
typedef struct
 {
   int hour;
   int minutes;
   int seconds;
 } time;
```

We can now declare variables to be of these new types as follows:

```
                    typedef node *NODEPTR;
                    struct node
                        {
                            int data;
                            NODEPTR next;
                        };
                    struct node node1,node2;
                    . . .
                    node1.data = 3, node2.data = -4;
                    node1.next = &node2, node2.next = NULL;
```

FIGURE 7.1 Two nodes of a linked list

```
    integer i;
    real n;
    string s;
    char_pointer buffer;
    time times[50];
```

7.2 LINKED LISTS

Elements of a *linked list* are often called *nodes*. Each node of the linked list contains a pointer to the next node. We can create and traverse a linked list by means of these pointers. The data structure used to create the nodes is the type struct with fields containing data and one field containing a pointer. To store integers in a linked list we might use the structure shown in Figure 7.1.

Note that node2.next is the NULL pointer, a special value indicating the end of the linked list. The constant NULL is defined in several of the standard header files, including stddef.h. (More on header files in the next chapter.)

To add a node to the list we use the function malloc, which returns a pointer to a segment of memory allocated for a struct node. Dynamic data structures give us the freedom to allocate memory as we need it. The function in Figure 7.2 will insert a node into a linked list.

7.3 BINARY TREES

A *binary tree* is a special linked list whose elements are stored nonsequentially, but sorted. Figure 7.3 show a binary tree. The tree begins with a root node that

7.3 BINARY TREES

```
int insert_after(NODEPTR prev, int value)
/* function to insert a node after the node pointed to
   by prev.  Return 0 if malloc fails, 1 otherwise.*/
{
 NODEPTR new;
 char *malloc();

 if ( (new = (NODEPTR)malloc(sizeof(struct node))) != 0)
 {
  new -> data = value;
  new -> next = prev -> next;
  prev -> next = new;
 }
 return( new != NULL );
}
```

FIGURE 7.2 Function to insert a node into a linked list

```
typedef struct node *NODEPTR
struct node
{
    int data;
    NODEPTR left,right;
};
```

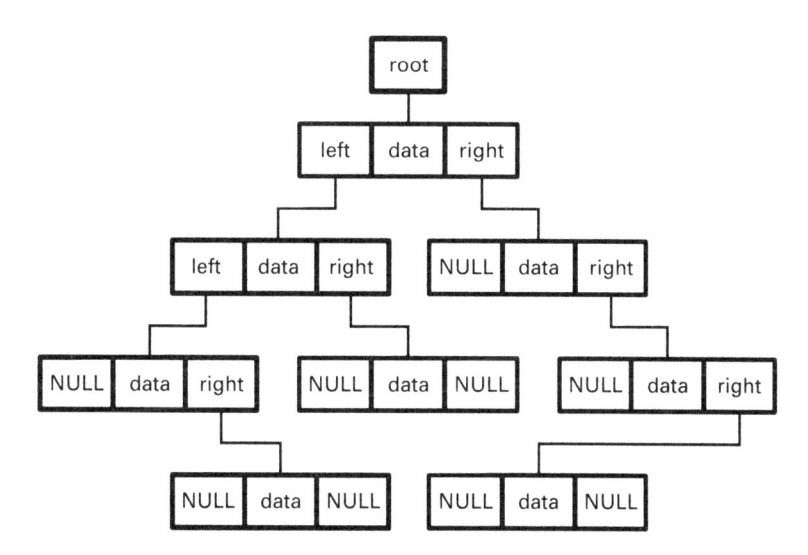

FIGURE 7.3 A binary tree model

Program 7.1

```
/*Program to read, sort and print a list of integers
 *using a binary tree.*/
#include <stdio.h>
#include <stdlib.h>

typedef struct node *NODEPTR;
struct node
{
int data;
NODEPTR left,right;
};

NODEPTR insert(int number, NODEPTR root)
/* function to insert number into a binary tree.  The
   pointer root is the root of the subtree which will
   contain number.*/
{
 if (root == NULL)
 { /* We have reached the bottom of the tree */
  root=calloc(1,sizeof (struct node));
  root->data = number;
  root->left = root->right = NULL;
 }
 else if (number > root->data)
  root->right = insert(number, root->right);
 else
  root->left = insert(number,root->left);

 return root;
}

void print_tree(NODEPTR root)
{
 if(root != NULL)
 {
  print_tree(root->left);
  printf("%d ",root->data);
  print_tree(root->right);
 }
}
```

FIGURE 7.4 (continues next page)

contains one data element and pointers to left and right subtrees, which are, recursively, binary trees (or empty). Nodes without any branches are called *leaves*. A node is a descendant of an ancestor node if it is in the left or right branch of the ancestor node.

Figure 7.4 illustrates some of the concepts we have covered in this chapter.

```
main()
{
 int i;
 NODEPTR root = 0;
 printf("Enter integers, end with a noninteger\n");
 while (scanf("%d",&i) > 0)
  root = insert(i, root);
 printf("The integers sorted are:\n");
 print_tree(root);
}
```

Program 7.1 output
```
Enter integers ending with a noninteger.
2 7 -3 6 -13 7 0 9 a
The integers sorted are:
-13 -3 0 2 6 7 7 9
```

FIGURE 7.4 Program to illustrate dynamic data structures

We include the header file `stdlib.h` in order to use the function `calloc`, which is analogous to `malloc` except that it allows more than one block of storage of the indicated size to be allocated. The insert and the print functions are both recursive.

EXERCISES

1. Write a program that creates a linked list with one node containing the time of the day. The time should indicate the following: 'A' for A.M. or 'P' for P.M.; the hour and the minutes. This initial node should contain time 0:0 A.M. and is known as the dummy header.

2. Add a function to the above program (exercise 1) that will insert a node, in correct order, into the above linked list. Invoke this function to insert three new nodes into the list. Hint: Use the function in Figure 7.2.

3. Add a function to the above program (exercise 1) that will print the linked list.

4. Add a function to the above program (exercise 1) to delete a given node from the linked list.

5. Add a recursive function to the Program in Figure 7.4 to print the data in each node together with the number of descendants of the node. The data need not be printed in order.

8
THE PREPROCESSOR

Before a source C program is compiled, it is processed by another program called the *preprocessor*. This gives the programmer the opportunity to customize the language to meet specific needs. The programmer can define constants and macros and include source files. All preprocessor statements begin with the symbol # and can appear anywhere in the program.

8.1 MACRO DEFINITIONS

We can use the `#define` statement to define constants.

```
#define TRUE 1
#define MAX 1000
#define PI 3.141592654
#define int_size 16
```

Whenever one of these defined names, or macros, is used, the equivalent value will be substituted. The only exception is inside a character string. So in the following declaration the value 1000 is not substituted for the string MAX:

```
char *ptr = "MAX";
```

The use of macros allows us to define a constant once instead of at every occurrence and to change it only once when we need to. It also helps program portability, since we can define constants such as integer size depending on the machine we are using.

The body of the definition need not be a constant. It may be an expression or any other text that is valid in C. For example, the following are all legitimate.

```
#define MOD %
#define NOT !
#define RIGHT_SHIFT_5 >>5
#define TWICE  2*
#define GREETING "Hello! How are you?"
```

These may be used as follows:

```
printf(GREETING);
if( NOT (x MOD 3 == 0))
  x = TWICE x;
```

The preprocessor stores the defining text without interpreting or evaluating it in any way. This allows us to define one macro in terms of another and in any order we wish.

We can also define macros that take one or more arguments. For example, AREA returns the area of the circle with the given radius.

```
#define AREA(r) ( PI * r * r )
#define MIN(x,y) ( (x) < (y) ? (x) : (y) )
```

then we can write

```
a = AREA( x );
l = MIN ( a + b , c) / 100;
```

Note that the parentheses around the definition of MIN and around the arguments ensure the proper evaluation of this expression.

Using macros rather than functions has some advantages, especially for simple functions. For example, in the above MIN macro we did not need to define types for the arguments x and y. They may be of type `int`, `float` or even `pointer`.

In fact we can pass a type as an argument to a macro, which we may not do with a function. The following macro prints data of different types depending on the argument passed to it.

```
#define print(type,data) \
       printf(#data "= %" #type "\n",data)
```

The backslash at the end of the line informs the preprocessor that the definition of print continues on the next line. The operator # creates a string literal from the text of the actual argument. For example:

```
print(d,length);
```

becomes

```
printf("length = %d\n", length);
```

There are, however, disadvantages to using macros, especially when the definition is lengthy. The code for a function appears only once in the program, but the code for a macro appears every time it is called. The macro code is simply substituted for the name on every call. This substitution may increase program size considerably for lengthy macros.

8.2 FILE INCLUSION

In C it is possible to include a file, usually called a header file, by using one of the following statements:

```
#include <filename>
#include "filename"
```

These files normally contain definitions that are needed in several source files. The <filename> form indicates that a system header file is being included, hence the system files are searched. The "filename" form indicates that the file is a customized file created by the programmer, and the current directory will be searched first. Some examples of system header files are the following:

```
#include <stdio.h>
#include <math.h>
```

or we may create our own file called logic.h using

```
#define TRUE 1
#define FALSE 0
#define AND &&
#define OR ||
#define NOT !
```

and

```
#include "logic.h"
```

The preprocessor will copy the contents of the file into the program at the point where the `#include` appears. It is therefore customary to include files at the beginning of the program before any reference to the contents of the file is made.

8.3 CONDITIONAL COMPILATION

The C preprocessor selects different sections of the source file for compilation, usually depending on the value of certain macros. *Conditional compilation* is often used to make programs more portable and to help with debugging. If we want to store integer values in a variable of type `int` or `long` depending on the machine, we could do something like the following:

```
#define IBMPC 8086™
#define VAX 11
#if MACHINE == VAX™
typedef int integer
  . . .
#elif MACHINE == IBMPC
typedef long integer
  . . .
```

```
#else
#error UNSPECIFIED MACHINE
 /* The preprocessor will output the above
    text and terminate compilation */
#endif
```

If we are using the IBM PC™ then we include

```
#define MACHINE IBMPC
```

The conditional compilation is often used as a debugging tool. If we wish to switch on and off certain statements for the purpose of debugging, we could define the macro DEBUG and use it as follows:

```
#define DEBUG
...
#if defined DEBUG
 printf ...
#endif
```

Once the program is successfully debugged, the statement defining DEBUG is removed (or placed inside a comment).

Finally we have the option of undefining names by using

```
#undef DEBUG
```

which will cause the definition DEBUG to be removed from the system.

EXERCISES

1. Define a macro MAX to find the maximum of two values.
2. Write a macro IS_DIGIT that gives a nonzero value if the character argument is in the range '0' - '9'.
3. Write a macro to swap two data items. These data items could be of type `int`, `float` or `char`. Write two calls to the macro using both an `int` and `float` type.

9
TURBO C

To enter the Turbo C environment from DOS, type "tc" and press Enter. What will appear on the screen is the Turbo C Main menu and the `Edit` window.

9.1 THE MENU

The TC file menu consists of eight choices:

    File Edit Run Compile Project Options Debug Break/watch

To toggle between the `Edit` window and the Main menu, use the TC hot key F10. See Appendix E for a list of other TC hot keys.

The File Menu

To use the `File` pull down menu, either press Alt-F or use the arrow key to move to the option and press Enter. The File menu has the following options:

File/Load	Type the name of the file you wish to use. F3 is a shortcut for the `File/Load` command.
File/Pick	Shows the list of the eight most recently edited files. The file chosen is loaded into the Editor and the cursor is placed at the location where you last edited the file.
File/New	Tells the editor that the file is a new file. The default file name is NONAME.C.
File/Save	Saves the file in the Editor to disk. F2 is a shortcut for the `File/Save` command and can be used from anywhere in the system to save your file.
File/Write	Prompts a file name and writes the file in the Editor to that file. This command overwrites existing files.

`File/Directory`   Displays the directory. Use F4 to change the wildcard mask.

`File/Change Dir`   Changes to a specified drive and directory.

`File/OS Shell`   Leaves TC temporarily and takes you to DOS. To return to TC type `EXIT`.

`File/Quit`   Quit TC and return to `DOS`.

The Edit Command

To use the built-in screen editor, press Alt-E or move to the menu using F10, move the cursor to Edit and press Enter.

While in the insert mode you can enter code in the `Edit` window. If you enter more than 77 characters on a line, the window scrolls as you type. To end a line you press Enter. Here are some of the most-used `Editor` commands.

Move the cursor through your text with the Up/Down, Left/Right arrows, and PgUp/PgDn keys.

Word left Ctrl-A
Word right Ctrl-F
Beginning of line Home
End of line End
Beginning of file Ctrl-PgUp
End of File Ctrl-PgDn
Delete a line with Ctrl-Y
Delete to end of line Ctrl-Q Y
Delete a word with Ctrl-T
Mark a block with Ctrl-K B(beginning) and Ctrl-K K(end)
Move a block with Ctrl-K V
Copy a block with Ctrl-K C
Delete a block with Ctrl-K Y
Read a block from disk Ctrl-K W
Write a block to disk Ctrl-K I

The Run Menu

The `Run` menu is used to run programs and to start and end debugging sessions. Except for the `Run/Run` command, all other commands on this menu are meant to be used with programs that have been compiled with the `Debug/Source` Debugging toggle set to On.

Run/Run Runs your program. It uses the arguments passed to it with the `Options/Arguments`. If the code has been modified since the last compilation, `Project Make` recompiles and links the program. If the `Debug/Source` Debugging toggle is set to `None`, the executable code will not contain any debugging information.

If the `Debug/Source` Debugging toggle is set to On, then if the program has not been modified since the last compilation, the `Run/Run` command causes the program to run to the next breakpoint or the end of the program if no breakpoints are set. For a discussion of breakpoints, see the `Break/Watch` Menu.

If the program has been modified and you are using the Step Over or the Trace Into, then the `Run/Run` will either recompile or run to the next step according to your response. If you are not stepping through the program, it is recompiled and will run from the beginning. The hot key for `Run/Run` is Ctrl-F9.

Program Reset The `Run/Program Reset` cancels the current debugging session. The hot key for `Run/Program Reset` is Ctrl-F2.

Go to Cursor This command advances the execution bar to the part of your program you wish to debug. Breakpoints can be set as needed. The hot key for the `Run/Go` to Cursor is F4.

Trace Into Use this command to move the execution position into a function called by the function you are now debugging.

This command causes you to step through each function line by line. The hot key for the `Run/Trace` command is F7.

Step Over Use this command to run the function you are now debugging one step at a time. This command suppresses the details of each function call and treats them as if they were single statements. The hot key for the `Run/Step Over` command is F8.

User Screen To examine output, Choose the **Run/User Screen** or the hot key Alt-5.

The Compile Menu

Compile to OBJ Compile the .C file to .OBJ file. The hot key for this command is Alt-F9.

Make EXE FILE Invokes Project Make to create .EXE file. The hot key for this command is F9.

Link Exe File Links the .OBJ and .LIB files to create a new .EXE file.

Build All Rebuilds all the files in your project.

Primary C File When the .C file includes headers(.H) files, the .H file with an error is loaded into the editor for correction.

Get Info Gives information about current file.

The Project Menu

The `Project` menu is used for combining multiple source and object files to create one executable file.

Project Name You choose the name to be given to the .EXE file. A common extension is .PRJ.

Break Make on Allows you to specify the default condition for stopping Make.

Auto Dependencies If this toggle is On, then when recompiling a source, those files used to build the .Obj file are checked and only recompiled if they have been modified.

Clear Project Clears the project name and resets the window.

Remove Messages Clears error messages from the Message window.

The Options Menu

The *Options menu* allows you to tailor the environment to your needs. It contains settings for the compiler, the linker, library and include directories, and program run-time arguments. Since these settings are normally used by the more experienced programmer, we refer the reader to the [Borland88, p. 112].

The Debug Menu

The *Debug menu* commands control the integrated debugger. We will not discuss all commands on this menu. To use the debugger it is important to check to see that the integrated debugging switch is on. This switch is normally set to on.

Debug/Evaluate Allows you to modify the value of a variable. The hot key for this command is Ctrl-F4.

The Break/Watch Menu

The commands in the *Break/Watch* menu are used to control breakpoints and watch expressions. A *breakpoint* is a place where you wish the execution of the program to stop in order for you to examine variables and expressions. You can examine these variables and expressions through the watch window. You can indicate the variables and expressions you wish to appear in the watch window by using the Add Watch command from this menu.

Add Watch You can add the name of a variable or an expression to the watch window by using this command. *Add Watch* enables you to watch the change of the values of variables as your program is running. You can add to the watch window at any time. When you choose this command, the debugger opens a window and prompts you to enter a watch expression. The default expression is the word at the cursor in the Edit window. When you type an expression and press Enter, Turbo C adds it to the watch window. The hot key for this command is Ctrl-F7.

Delete Watch This command deletes the current expression from the watch window. The watch window must be visible to use this command. If you want to delete a watch expression that is not current, you must go to the watch window and move the cursor to that watch expression and press Del.

Edit Watch This command allows you to edit the watch window.

Remove All Watches This command deletes all watches from the watch window.

Toggle Breakpoint This command sets or clears breakpoints. You can mark lines in your program as stop points. When you run a program, it stops at the first breakpoint. You can then examine the expressions in the watch window. From this point on, you can step through the program by using the F7 key. You may set as many breakpoints as you wish.

Clear All Breakpoint This command clears all breakpoints.

View Next Breakpoint This command will move the cursor to the next breakpoint in the order that the breakpoints were set.

A Debugging Session

This debugging session will enable you to use some of the features of an integrated debugger to debug the following simple program. Start by using the Turbo C™ Editor to create the following source file:

```
float average(float x[],int n)
/* compute the average of x[0], ..., x[n-1]*/
{
 int i;
 double sum = 0;
 for (i = 0; i < n; ++i)
  sum += x[i];
 return sum/n;
}

main()
{
   int n,i=0;
   float x[10];
/*1*/ printf("How many (<10) numbers to average?\n");
   scanf("%d", &n);
/*2*/ printf("Enter the numbers:\n");
   for ( i = 0; i < n; i++)
   scanf("%f", &x[i]);

/*3*/ printf("The average is %f\n", average(x,n));
}
```

After saving the source file, place the cursor on line 1 and press F10 followed by R to reach the run commands. Move the cursor to Go To Cursor and press Enter. You have initiated the debugging session. The program execution will stop at the cursor. Press F10 followed by B to reach the Break/Watch commands. The cursor should be on the Add Watch command. Press Enter. A window will open to the word your cursor was on. Now enter the variables you will watch as the program executes. Type i followed by Enter and the variable i appears on the watch window. Press F10, Enter, Enter to add x[1], then press Enter. Again press F10, Enter, Enter, and type x[0],3 followed by Enter; this will show the first three values of your array x.

Now you are ready to add the breakpoints. Move the cursor to line 2 and press Enter. Move the cursor to Toggle Breakpoint and press Enter. Press F10 followed by R followed by Enter (or hot key Ctrl-F9). The program execution will now stop at the first breakpoint, which should be line 2. Press F7 and enter how many data you want to average, for example 3. Press F7 to step through the program, observing the watch window for changes until you reach line 3.

We will now use the Debug/Evaluate command to change the value of x[1]. Press F10, then D, followed by Enter. Type x[1], bring the cursor to New value, type the new value, and press Enter and observe the new value in the Result window. Press F10 twice to see the result in the watch window. Now you are back on line 3. If you want to step over the function average, press F8; otherwise press F7. When you have finished executing the program, press Ctrl-F2 (Run/Program Reset) to cancel the current debugging session.

9.2 TURBO C CHARACTER GRAPHICS

gotoxy, clrscr

We can use the `gotoxy` function to direct output to a desired region of the screen. The top left-hand corner of the screen has coordinates (1,1). The bottom right-hand corner of the fullscreen is (80,25). The `gotoxy` function is included in the `<conio.h>` library. This function is useful in such areas as drawing figures on the screen, since it allows us to back up. It is also used to move the cursor in such a way as to facilitate the input of data. For example, Program 4.4 requested information about students to be input. If we create column headings and move the cursor to appropriate locations on the screen, the data input is facilitated. We rewrite Program 4.3 as shown in Figure 9.1 (see next page).

To use the `gotoxy` function, it is useful to know where the cursor is at any time. The following functions serve to supply information:

wherex   Gives the x_coordinate (column position) of the cell containing the cursor.

wherey   Gives the y_coordinate (row position) of the cell containing the cursor.

Windows

A *window* is a rectangular area defined on the PC's video screen when it is in text mode. When the program writes to the screen, its output is restricted to the active window. It is possible to change the active window with the `window` function.

```
window(6,3,30,15)
```

will limit output to the box with top-left corner positioned at column 6, row 3 and the bottom right-hand position at column 30, row 15. To output to the window, the `cprintf` and `cputs` functions are used.

EXERCISES

1. The following program is intended to perform matrix multiplication. Use the features of the Turbo C™ interactive debugger to debug the program.

   a. Use the Turbo C editor to create the following file.

Program 9.1
```
#include <conio.h>
#define MAX_STUDENTS 30 /*MAX_STUDENTS is a constant for the
maximum number of students*/
main()
/* This program will ask as input the college GPA and student
   records, and will output them.*/
{
 int j,i = 0;
 struct student
 {
  char name[15];
       /* There are at most 15 characters in a name */
  int credits;
  float GPA;
  char gender;
 };
 struct student class[MAX_STUDENTS];
              /* class is an array of students */
 float college_GPA;
 clrscr();
 gotoxy(1,1);  /*Move to top left-hand corner*/
 printf("Enter the college GPA.\n");
 scanf("%f",&college_GPA);
 printf("Enter students, Z to terminate.\n");
 gotoxy(5,5);  /* move to row 5 column 5 for heading.*/
 printf("    name        credits   GPA   sex\n");
 for (i = 0; i < MAX_STUDENTS; ++i)
 {
  gotoxy(5,7+i);
  /*increase row number by i for each student.*/
  scanf("%15s", class[i].name);
  if(class[i].name[0] == 'Z' ||class[i].name[0] == 'z')
   break;
  gotoxy(24,7+i);
  scanf("%d",&class[i].credits);
  gotoxy(32,7+i);
  scanf("%f",&class[i].GPA);
  gotoxy(38,7+i);
  scanf(" %c",&class[i].gender);
 }
 printf("The college grade point average is: %5.2f\n",
 college_GPA);
 printf("    name        credits   GPA   sex\n");
 for( j = 0; j < i; ++j)
 {
  printf("%-15s    %3d   ",
         class[j].name,class[j].credits);
W  printf("%5.2f   %c\n",class[j].GPA,class[j].gender);
 }
}
```

FIGURE 9.1 (continues next page)

Program 9.1 Output

```
Enter the college GPA.
2.3
Enter students, Z to terminate.
    name         credits    GPA   sex
Henry-Williams     45       2.7    m
Joan-Smith         87       3.2    f
z
The college grade point average is:  2.30
    name         credits    GPA   sex
Henry-Williams     45       2.70   m
Joan-Smith         87       3.20   f
```

FIGURE 9.1 Program to illustrate character graphics

```
main()
{
  int a[4][3] = { {7, 3, 0},
                  {5, 3, 7},
                  {-1, 6, 0},
                  {9, 4, 6} };
  int b[3][2] = { {8, 3},
                  {4, 0},
                  {2, 5} };
  int c[4][2],i,j,k;

  for(i =1; i<4 ; i++)
    for(j =1; j< 2; j++)
      for(k = 1; k < 3; k++)
        c[i][j] += a[i][k]*b[k][j];

  for(i = 1; i < 4; i++)
  {
    for(j = 1; j < 2; j ++)
      printf("%4d",c[i][j]);
    printf("\n");
  }
}
```

    b. Use the Turbo Debugger to correct this program and verify that the program works correctly.

2. Use the following character graphics functions `window`, `gotoxy`, and `cputs` to open a window in approximately the middle of the screen. Display the contents of an external file in that window. The name of the file to be displayed should be a command line argument. When the window is full, the program should wait for the user to press Enter before resuming output.

10
INTRODUCTION TO C++

C++ is an extension of C that implements many of the ideas of *object-oriented programming (OOP)*. In these few pages it would be impossible to review, even in broad outline, the fundamental ideas of object-oriented programming. Suffice it to say that they require a software development paradigm which differs substantially from traditional methods. In this brief introduction to C++ we will see only a glimpse of the primary device of this new paradigm.

As its name implies, objects are the central focus of program development in an object-oriented language. In brief, an object in C++ comprises a set of data items and a set of functions. Normally, an application does not reference the data items directly; rather, access to them is made through the member functions. In this way, the implementation of an object such as a queue can be encapsulated as one unit.

10.1 CLASSES

An object is implemented in C++ by extending the structure data type to include functions as structure members. Additional keywords control access to the structure or `class` members. (A `class` is a new data type that is almost identical to a struct, differing only in the default access type.)

Figure 10.1 shows the definition of `class` fraction. An object of type fraction is simply a pair of integers (the numerator and denominator of a fraction). The class includes functions that define the standard arithmetic functions for fractions. Thus the following statements are valid.

```
class fraction {
private:
  long top; // numerator
  unsigned long bottom; //denominator
   static unsigned long gcd(unsigned long, unsigned long);
  fraction & reduce(); //to lowest terms
  fraction & init(long numerator, long denominator);
 public:
  fraction(long numerator=0, long denominator=1) {
   init(numerator, denominator);
  }

  long numerator() const { return top; }
  long denominator() const { return bottom; }

  fraction & reset(long numerator, long denominator=1) {
   //replace old fraction with a new one
   return init(numerator, denominator);
  }

  operator long () const { return top / (long)bottom;}

  fraction operator - () const {
   fraction temp(-top, bottom);
   return temp;
  }

  fraction operator + (const fraction & a) const;
  fraction operator - (const fraction & a) const {
   return operator + (-a);
  }

  fraction operator * (const fraction & a) const {
   fraction temp(top*a.top, bottom*a.bottom);
   return temp;
  }
```

FIGURE 10.1 (continues next page)

```
    fraction f1(2,3);   // The fraction 2/3
    fraction f2(4);     // The fraction 4/1
    fraction f3,f4;     // No value specified; defaults to 0/1
    f3 = -7;
    f4 = f2 + f1*(f3 + 5);
    printf("f4 =");  f4.print();  // output: f4 = 8/3
```

Several aspects of this example require explanation. Note, first of all, that C++ includes an additional comment format: "//" begins a comment which extends to the end of the line.

The definition of a `class` is often quite large. Normally the class definition is placed in a separate "header file" and included in any module using this

```
fraction operator / (const fraction & a) const {
  fraction temp(top*(long)a.bottom,
                a.top*(long)bottom);
  return temp;
  }
int operator < (const fraction & a) const {
  return top*(long)a.bottom < a.top*(long)bottom;
  }
int operator <=  (const fraction & a) const {
  return top*(long)a.bottom <= a.top*(long)bottom;
  }
int operator > (const fraction & a) const {
  return ! operator <= (a);
  }
int operator >= (const fraction & a) const {
  return ! operator < (a);
  }
void print() const {
  printf("%ld/%lu", top, bottom);
  }
};
```

FIGURE 10.1 Definition of class fraction

`class` through the preprocessor directive `#include`. In this example we would use

```
#include "fraction.h"
```

The member functions that are declared but not defined in fraction.h are collected in another file called fraction.cpp. (The two "p's" are for "plus," as in C++.) Functions that are defined inside the `class` definition are, by default, `inline` functions. This means that the compiler need not generate the usual code for calling a function, but may instead insert the body of the function at the point where it is invoked. This makes sense only if the body of the function is very short. Furthermore, the `inline` qualifier is only a suggestion to the compiler; the compiler may ignore it.

Now we consider the definition of `class` fraction. The keyword `private` introduces `class` members which may be referenced only by other members (functions) of the `class`. In this case the numerator and denominator (called top and bottom to avoid confusion with the member functions numerator() and denominator()) are private to ensure that each fraction is always in lowest terms with a positive denominator. The member functions `gcd`, `reduce`, and `init` are private because they are needed only by other member functions.

10.2 CONSTRUCTORS

A member function with the same name as the `class` name (i.e., fraction in this example) is called a *constructor*. Each time an object of any type is created, an appropriate constructor is invoked. A constructor is a special function that typically initializes data items, allocates memory if required, etc. A constructor may not contain a `return` statement (and hence its definition may not specify a return value). The idea is to ensure that an object is in a usable state as soon as it is created. In class fraction the constructor need assign values only to top and bottom and ensure that they are in lowest terms.

The constructor for `class` fraction utilizes another new feature of C++, namely the specification of default values for function parameters. In general a function may have zero or more required arguments (no defaults) followed by zero or more arguments, each with a default value. The constructor for `class` fraction may thus be invoked with zero, one or two arguments. Since the second argument defaults to 1, this allows a fraction to be assigned an integral initial value:

```
fraction f = 3;   //equivalent to fraction f(3);
```

10.3 MEMBER FUNCTIONS OF CLASS FRACTION

The member function `init` initializes (or reinitializes) a fraction. The function `gcd` computes the greatest common divisor of two positive integers, which is required by the function reduce to "divide out" any common factor of the numerator and denominator.

The functions numerator() and denominator() give "read-only" access to the fraction.

The function reset is used to assign a new value to a fraction. Thus

```
f1 = f2.reset(1);
```

sets both f1 and f2 to the fraction 1/1. The return type for reset, fraction &, is read "a reference to a fraction." We will discuss references only briefly. A *reference* is an alias for another variable and as such may be used as an rvalue or an lvalue. If we had used the declaration

```
long & numerator() { return top; }
```

(so that the return type is a reference to a `long`), then the assignment

```
f1.numerator() = 7;
```

would be legal and would change f1.top to 7.

The remaining functions in class fraction extend the standard arithmetic operators to handle fraction operands. The syntax for doing this may seem strange at first glance. For example, to define the product of two fractions, as in f1 * f2, the following function is defined:

```
fraction operator *(const fraction &f) const {
  fraction temp(top*f.top, bottom*f.bottom);
  return temp;
}
```

The name of this function is "`operator *`." It takes one argument, namely a fraction. The expression f1 * f2 is equivalent to `f1.operator*(f2)`. Within the body of this function, references to top and bottom are, in effect, references to f1.top and f1.bottom. This function simply returns a newly created fraction defined with the correct numerator and denominator.

The parameter f has type `const` fraction &. This means that f is an alias for the actual argument; in other words, the actual argument is passed by reference. This passing avoids the need to copy the object when the function is invoked. Since arguments are always passed by value in C, this mechanism for passing by reference is a feature of C++.

One final comment concerning this function. The two appearances of the qualifier `const` tell the compiler that the two fractions involved will not be changed within the body of the function.

Now, what about an expression such as f1*5 or 5*f1, where only one of the arguments is a fraction? Since f1*5 is equivalent to `f1.operator*(5)`, what is required for this to be valid is a cast (that is, a type conversion) from type `int` to type fraction. Such a cast is implicitly defined because an `int` may be converted to a `long` that may in turn be converted to a fraction. The reason a `long` may be converted to a fraction is that `class` fraction includes a constructor which accepts a single `long` argument.

Similarly, 5*f1 is valid because there is an explicit cast defined from class fraction to `long`, namely the member function `operator long`. (Without this explicit cast, the expression 5*f1 would be invalid.) Thus the results of 5*f1 (a `long` value) and f1*5 (a fraction) are quite different.

In **class** fraction there are two functions named "`operator -`":

```
fraction operator -() const;
fraction operator - (const fraction & a);
```

The first is the unary minus operator (applied to a fraction), and the second is the binary difference operator. This illustrates the fact that two functions with the same name are considered different functions in C++ if the number and/or types of arguments are different. One program could have, for example, two functions for averaging arrays:

```
float average(int a[], int n);
float average(float a[], int n);
```

It is primarily for this reason that a function must be declared before it is referenced. That is, function prototypes are essential in C++.

```
#include "fraction.h"

fraction fraction::operator + (const fraction &b) const
{
 unsigned long c = gcd(bottom,b.bottom);
 fraction temp;
 if (c == 0) { //one fraction has zero denominator
  temp.top = bottom == 0 ? top : b.top;
  temp.bottom = 0;   //indicates bad result
  return temp;
  }
// a1/a2 + b1/b2 = (a1*b2 + a2*b1)/ (a2*b2)
//                = (a1*b2/c + b1*a2/c) / (a2*b2/c),
// where c = gcd(a2, b2)
temp.top = top * (long)(b.bottom/c) + b.top * (long)(bottom/c);
temp.bottom = (bottom/c)*b.bottom;
return temp.reduce();
}
```

FIGURE 10.2 Definition of addition in `fraction.cpp`

As mentioned above, the file fraction.cpp contains the member functions of class fraction that are declared but not defined in the definition of `class` fraction. A part of this file, with the definition of the addition operator, is shown in Figure 10.2. The class name prefix—namely, fraction::—tells the compiler that this function is a member of `class` fraction. A member of a `class` or `struct` may always be qualified by such a prefix, which is employed to resolve potential ambiguity (or to access a function that is hidden in the current scope).

10.4 PROPERTIES OF CLASSES

This example illustrates two related properties of objects, namely *encapsulation* and *data hiding*. Encapsulation simply means that all the data and functions connected with an object are defined in one unit.

Data hiding allows the author of a `class` to hide implementation details from the user. For example, a `class` that implements a stack would have operations to add or remove the top of the stack. The particular method of maintaining the stack (as an array or linked list, for example) need not be known to the programmer using the stack `class`.

Object-oriented programming has two other important properties that are also features of C++: *inheritance* and *polymorphism*. Inheritance allows a class to be defined as an extension of one or more previously defined classes. The "derived" `class` inherits the members of the "base" `class` and includes additional members. (Member functions may be also be redefined in the derived class.) Thus one may construct hierarchies of classes in which more specific and concrete classes are built from the more abstract classes.

Polymorphism is the ability to share the same name for an action that has a different implementation for each class in a class hierarchy. For example, in a hierarchy of graphical objects, each object has a *draw action*. The implementation of the draw function for a circle might be quite different from that for a straight line segment. At execution time the particular draw function invoked is determined by the type of object referenced.

10.5 ANOTHER CLASS EXAMPLE

We will illustrate these ideas through two further examples. Figure 10.3 shows the definition of a class that implements a "safe" integer array. Safe means that any attempt to reference an element beyond the end of the array is detected. To declare an array of 10 elements:

```
array a1(10);
```

Values may be stored in the array in the usual way:

```
a1[3] = 7;
```

A reference to a1[20], however, will cause the program to abort.

This class has two constructors. The second one is the following:

```
array(const array &);
```

This is called the copy constructor because it is used to define an array as a copy of an existing array, as in

```
array a2 = a1;
```

A copy constructor is always implicitly defined. The default copy constructor merely copies the data items from the existing object to the newly created object. In cases where the creation of an object requires allocation of memory, it is usually necessary to provide an explicit copy constructor. In this case the copy constructor copies the array elements into newly allocated memory.

Since memory is allocated when an array is created, it must be deallocated when the array is destroyed. (Recall that a local variable is created when a function is entered and destroyed on exit from the function.) The *destructor* for a class is a function with the same name as the class but prefixed by a tilde. The destructor for class array calls free to release the memory allocated by the array constructor.

For the same reason that a copy constructor is defined, the assignment operator is overloaded. If a1 and a2 are arrays, then the assignment

```
a1 = a2;
```

```
#include <stdlib.h>
class array {
 private:
  unsigned nbr_elements;  // current length of array
  unsigned max_size;      // room for max_size elements
  int *elements; // the array itself

  array & init(unsigned initial_size, unsigned size = 1);
 protected:
  // insert and remove (an array member) can only be
  // used by derived classes:
  array & insert(unsigned i, int member);
  array & remove(unsigned i);

  // change the nbr of elements; realloc if necessary:
  array & resize(unsigned new_size);

  array & make_empty() {  // remove all elements
   nbr_elements = 0;
   return *this;
  }

  int & quit(unsigned i) const;  //see operator []
 public:
  // create an empty array :
  array(unsigned max_size=1) { init(max_size); }

  array(const array &);  // copy constructor

  ~array() {  // destroy an array
   free(elements);
  }

  unsigned size() const { return nbr_elements; }

  array & operator = (const array &);

  int & operator [](unsigned i) const {
   return i >= nbr_elements ? quit(i) : elements[i];
  }

  // compare two arrays:
  int operator == (const array &) const;
  int operator != (const array &a) const {
   return ! operator == (a);
  }

  virtual void
  print();
};
```

FIGURE 10.3 Class array

is equivalent to the function call

    a1.operator =(a2);

This function copies array elements from a2.elements to a1.elements.

The primary function in class array is the overloading of the *subscript operator* (`operator []`). The *overloaded operator* is equivalent to the usual subscript operator except that it checks for improper subscripts.

The last public function displays (on `stdout`) the elements of the array, separated by commas.

In addition to private and public members, this `class` contains `protected` members. A `protected` member may be referenced from within member functions of the same `class` and also from within a derived `class`. In other contexts a `protected` member, like a `private` member, may not be accessed. We will look at a derived `class` momentarily. In `class` array the `protected` members manipulate the array in ways that are not generally appropriate, but are required for other objects which are implemented using arrays. An example is `class` set, shown in Figure 10.4 (see next page).

10.6 A DERIVED CLASS

The `class` set (set of integers) is derived from `class` array, hence `class` array is the "base" `class` for `class` set. The derivation from `class` array is indicated on the first line:

    class array : public set {

The qualifier `public` means that the `public` members of the base class (i.e., class set) will also be `public` members of the derived `class` (unless redefined in the derived `class`). As mentioned above, the `protected` members of the base `class` may be accessed inside `class` array (although the `private` members may not). In the case at hand, the constructors for `class` set use the `protected` member insert to build an array in ascending order.

When a derived `class` is created, a constructor for the base `class` is invoked before the constructor of the derived `class`. If the default constructor is not appropriate, an explicit base `class` constructor may be specified. For example, the copy constructor for `class` set is

    set(const set &s) : array(s) {}

This indicates that the constructor array::array(const array &) (that is, the copy constructor for class array) should be invoked. The body is empty because the required initialization is performed by the base class constructor.

```
#include "array.h"

class set : public array {
 private:
  //cast an array to a set (simplifies binary operations):
  set (const array &a) : array(a) {}

  // find the position of 'e'.
  // Return TRUE if 'e' is an element of the set.
  int find_element(int e, unsigned &i) const;

 public:
  // create an empty set with room for 'size' elements;
  set(unsigned size=1) : array(size) { make_empty();}

  set(const set &s) : array(s) {} //copy constructor

  // create a set with one or more elements:
  set(unsigned count, int element, ...);

  // add 'count' elements to the set:
  set & add_elements(unsigned count, int element, ...);

  // return TRUE/FALSE if e is/is not in the set
  int is_element(int e) const {
   unsigned dummy;
   return find_element(e, dummy);
   }

  //  redefine operator [] so that, for example,
  //  s[i] = 3 is not possible:
  int operator [] (unsigned i) const {
   return array::operator [] (i);
   }

  set operator | (const set &s) const;   // set union

  set operator & (const set &s) const;   // intersection

  set operator - (const set &s) const;   // set difference

  int operator <= (const set &s) const;  // is a subset

  set & make_empty() {
   array::make_empty();
   return *this;
   }

  void print();
};
```

FIGURE 10.4 Class set

10.6 A DERIVED CLASS

Notice that in this constructor the set s is cast to an array in the call array(s). In general a variable of a derived `class` may always be cast to the base `class`. The reverse cast, base to derived, is invalid unless explicitly defined. This cast is defined for `class` set by the (private) constructor set::set(`const` array &).

In the member function make_empty is an example of the keyword `this`. The keyword `this` is a pointer to the object on which the member function operates. For example, in the call s.make_empty(), the value of `this` is &s.

A set of integers is represented as an *ascending array*. (This representation makes sense only if unions and intersections are performed frequently.) To maintain the ascending property, it must be impossible for the application code to alter a set element directly. On the other hand, the subscript operator defined in class array allows exactly that. Therefore, in class set, the subscript operator is redefined so that it returns an rvalue.

The print function is also redefined. The elements of the set are printed inside braces as in {1,2,3}. Notice that in class array the definition of the print function includes the qualifier `virtual`. To see the significance of this definition, consider the following code fragment:

```
array a1(3,1,2,3);   // the array 1,2,3
set s1(3,1,2,3);     // the set {1,2,3}
array *p;

p = &a1;
p->print();   //output:  1,2,3
p = &s1;
p->print();   //output:  {1,2,3}
```

Here p is a pointer to the base `class`; references via p to members of the base `class`, such as p->size(), refer unconditionally to array::size. Since the print function is `virtual`, however, the function actually referenced in p->print() depends on the class (base or derived) of the object currently pointed at by p.

The remainder of the `class` includes definitions of the standard set operations.

EXERCISES

1. Extend `class` set by adding the function

    ```
    set & set::operator |= (const set &s);
    ```

    which replaces *this by *this | s. That is, s1 |= s2 is equivalent to s1 = s1 | s2. Write a short program to test the new operator.

2. Define the `class` complex, which provides a representation of complex numbers z = x + iy. The real and imaginary parts x and y should be public members. The standard floating-point arithmetic operators should be overloaded to allow, for example, z1=z2+z3*z4, where z1, z2, z3, and z4

are all of class complex. Write a short program to test the member functions of your new class. Note: if z1 = x1 +iy1 and z2 = x2 +iy2, then

```
z1*z2 = (x1*x2 - y1*y2) + i(x2*y1 + x1*y2)
z1/z2 = ((x1*x2 + y1*y2) + i(x2*y1 - x1*y2)) / (x2*x2 + y2*y2)
```

3. Define the `class` n_tuple, which implements n-tuples of integers. An n-tuple is just an ordered list of n numbers. The class should be derived from class array. In addition to the operations derived from the base `class`, the `class` n_tuple should include the following:

```
int n_tuple::operator <= (const tuple &nt) const;
int n_tuple::operator < (const tuple &nt) const;
int n_tuple::print();
```

The operators <= and < allow two tuples to be compared using lexicographical ordering. Thus [6, 3, 5, 9] < [6, 4, 4, 1], while [6,3,5, 1] > [6, 3, 4, 9]. The function print should output the n-tuple using brackets. Note that n_tuple::print may invoke array::print.

A
LANGUAGE DESCRIPTION

This appendix contains a language description for C according to the new ANSI and ISO standard for C programming. All syntax diagrams are taken from [Plauger and Brodie, 1989] with their permission. A list of the valid C tokens and descriptions of the syntax of `declarations`, `function definitions`, and `expressions` are given. A C program consists of these constructs and preprocessor directives and macros.

C TOKENS

Keywords (Keywords have special meaning to the translator.)

auto	default	float	register	struct	volatile
break	do	for	return	switch	while
case	double	goto	short	typedef	
char	else	if	signed	union	
const	enum	int	sizeof	unsigned	
continue	extern	long	static	void	

We will use syntax diagrams to describe the language. A `name` C token has the syntax diagram shown in Figure A.1.

To create a `name` token you follow the arrows in the direction indicated. When you come to a box, you choose one of the forms and continue. When reaching an intersection, you may choose any arrow you like. So Figure A.1 indicates that a `name` token must begin with a letter or an underscore followed by as many digits, letters, or underscores as we want.

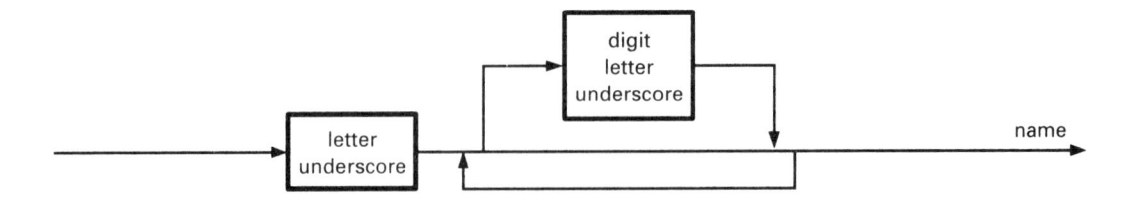

FIGURE A.1

INTEGER, FLOATING, CHARACTER CONSTANTS AND STRING LITERALS

Figures A.2–A.6 are syntax diagrams for these tokens.

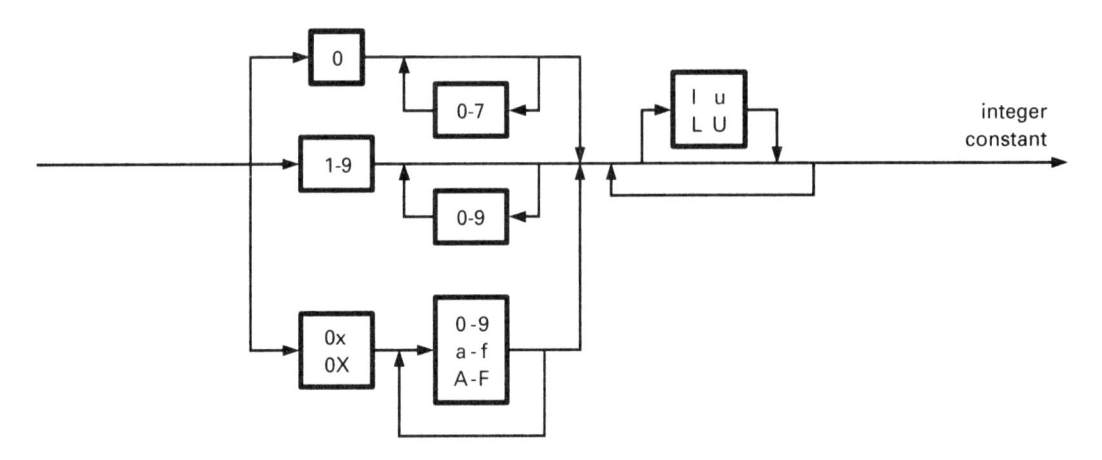

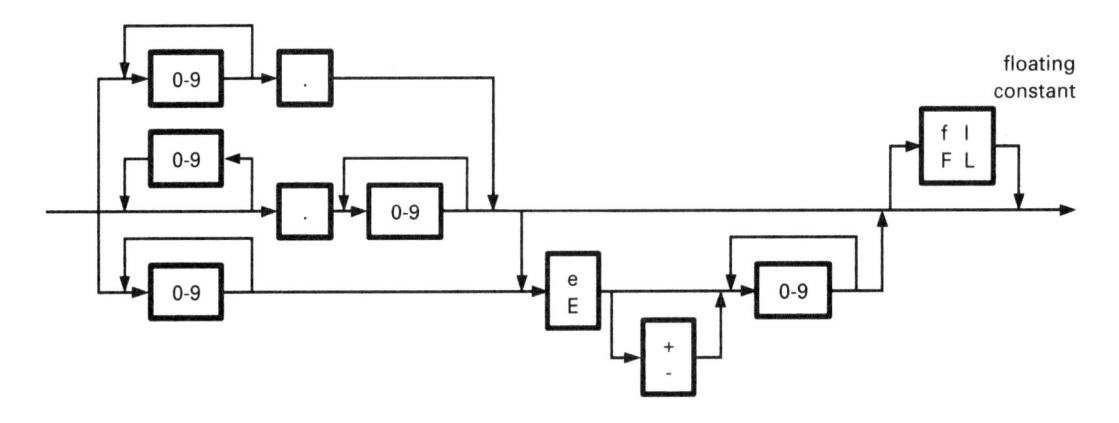

FIGURE A.2

FIGURE A.3

VALID OPERATOR **85**

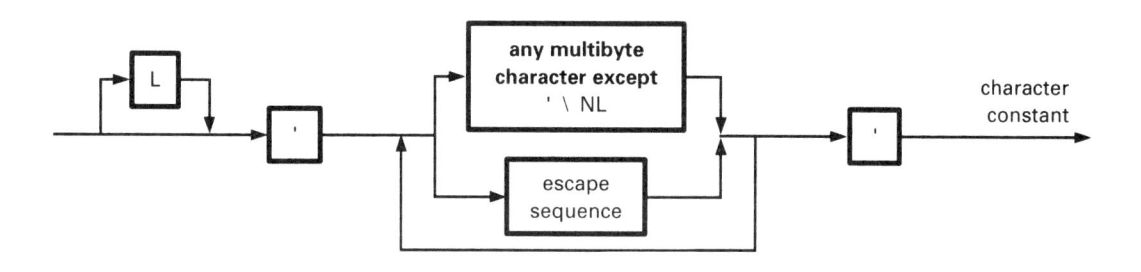

FIGURE A.4

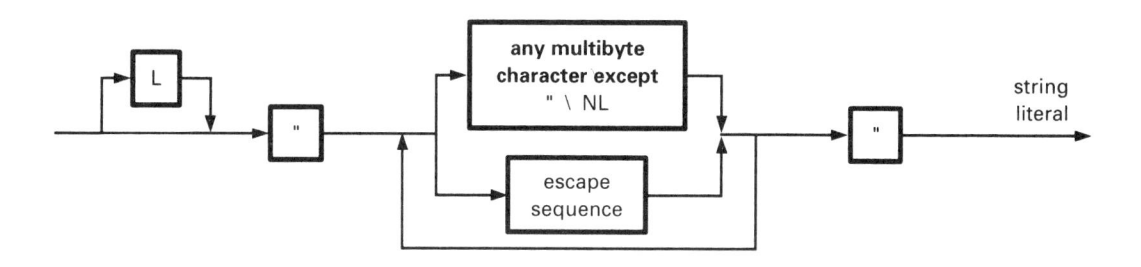

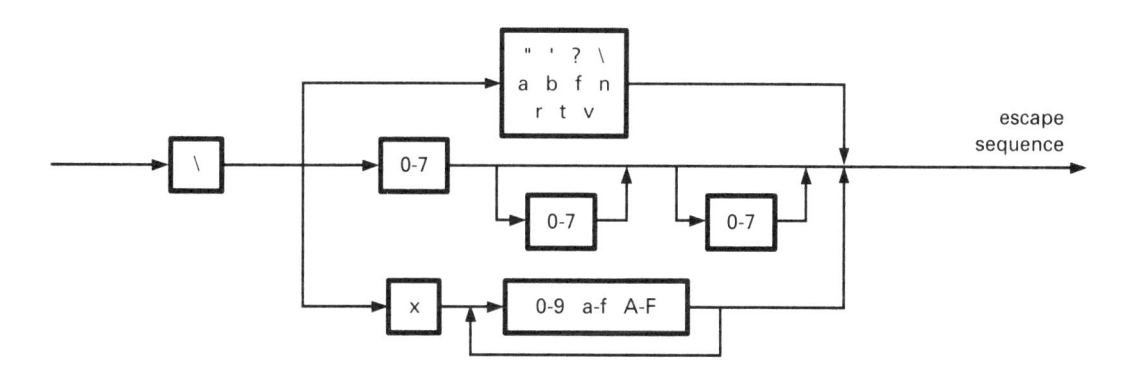

FIGURE A.5

FIGURE A.6

VALID OPERATOR

```
...    &&    -=    >=    -    +    ;    ]
<<=    &=    ->    >>    %    ,    <    ^
>>=    *=    /=    ^=    &    -    =    {
!=     ++    <<    |=    (    .    >    |
%=     +=    <=    ||    )    /    ?    }
       --    ==    !     *    :    [
```

DECLARATION SYNTAX

The translator parses all C tokens in a translation unit into one or more declarations, some of which are function definitions. Declarations can contain other declarations. You cannot write a function definition inside another declaration.

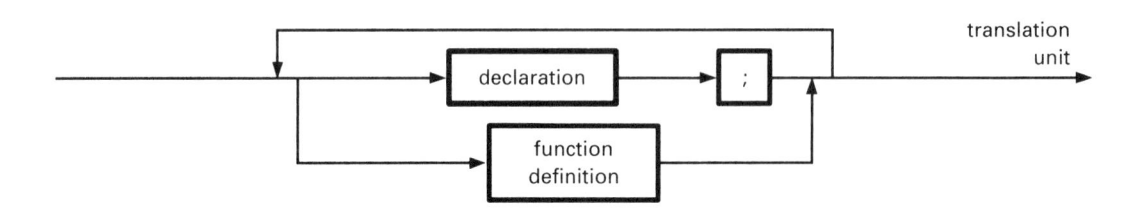

FIGURE A.7

A Declaration Other than a Function Definition

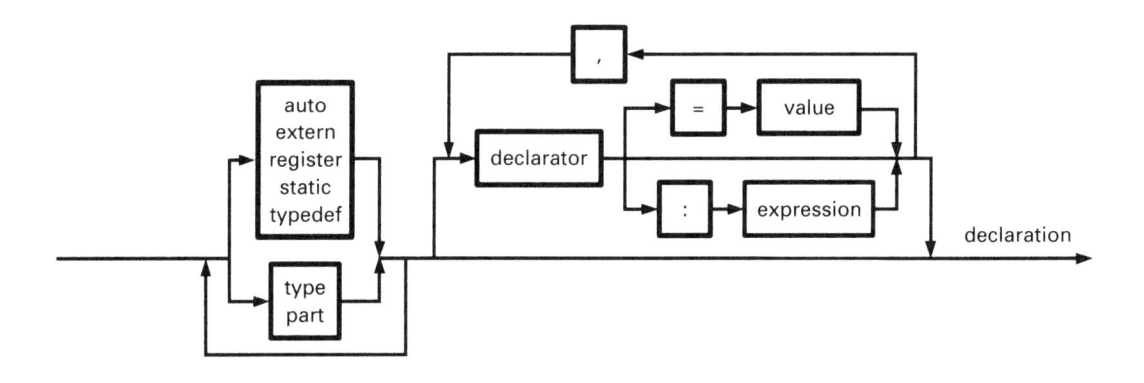

FIGURE A.8

DECLARATION SYNTAX

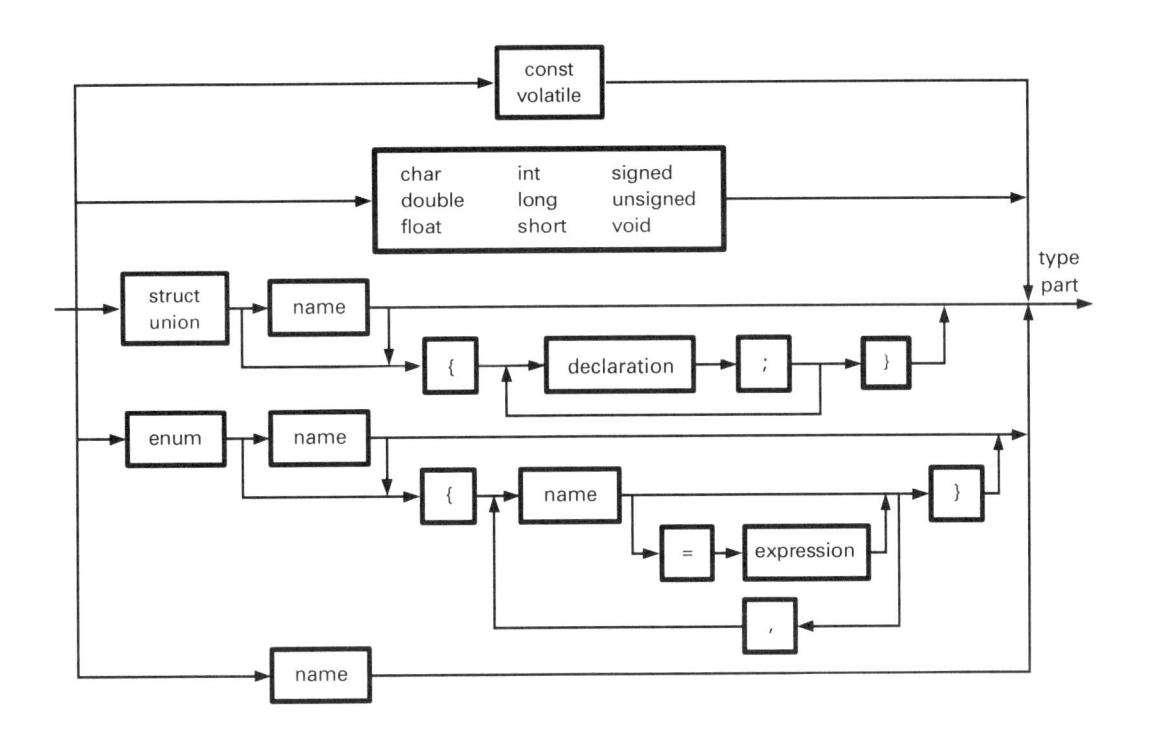

FIGURE A.9

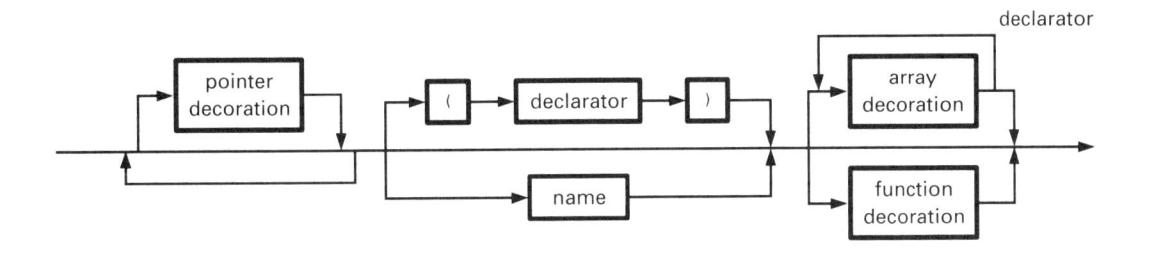

FIGURE A.10

88 APPENDIX A LANGUAGE DESCRIPTION

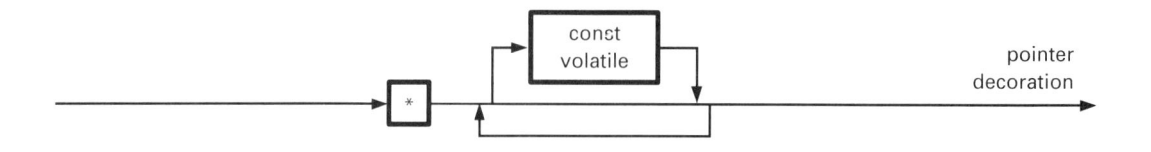

FIGURE A.11

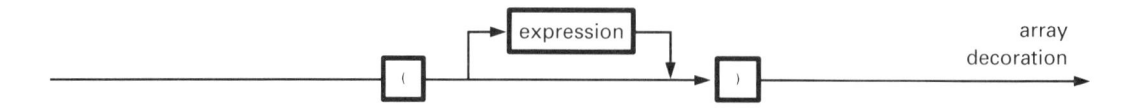

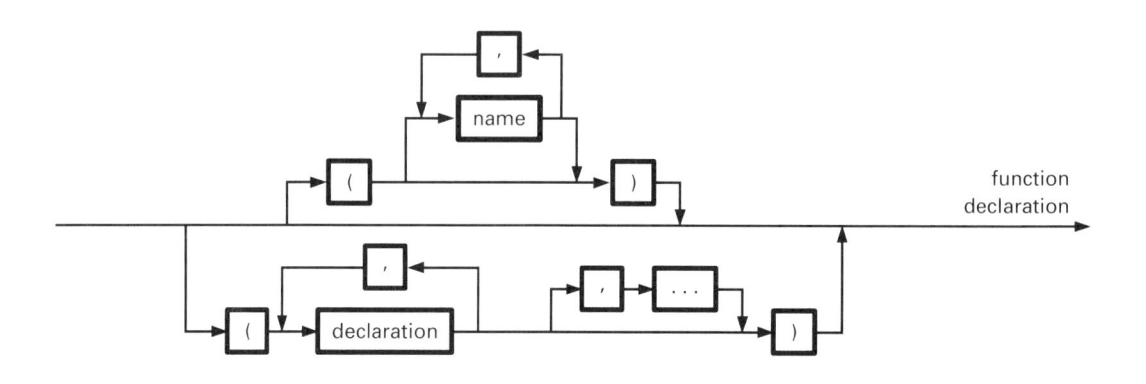

FIGURE A.12

FIGURE A.13

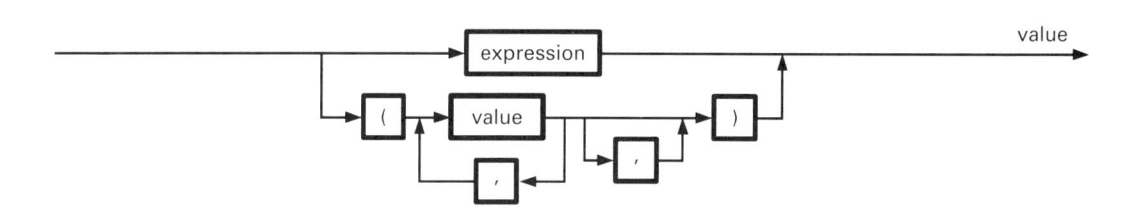

FIGURE A.14

FUNCTION DEFINITION

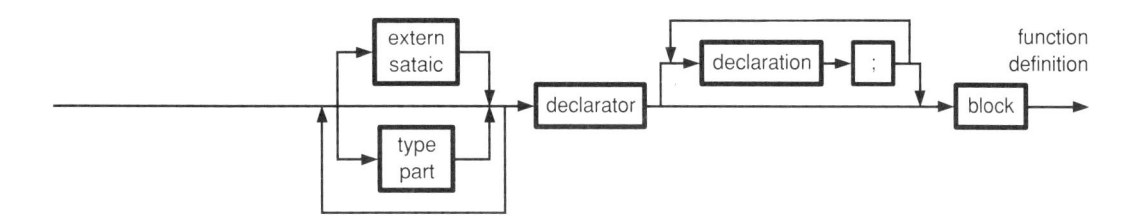

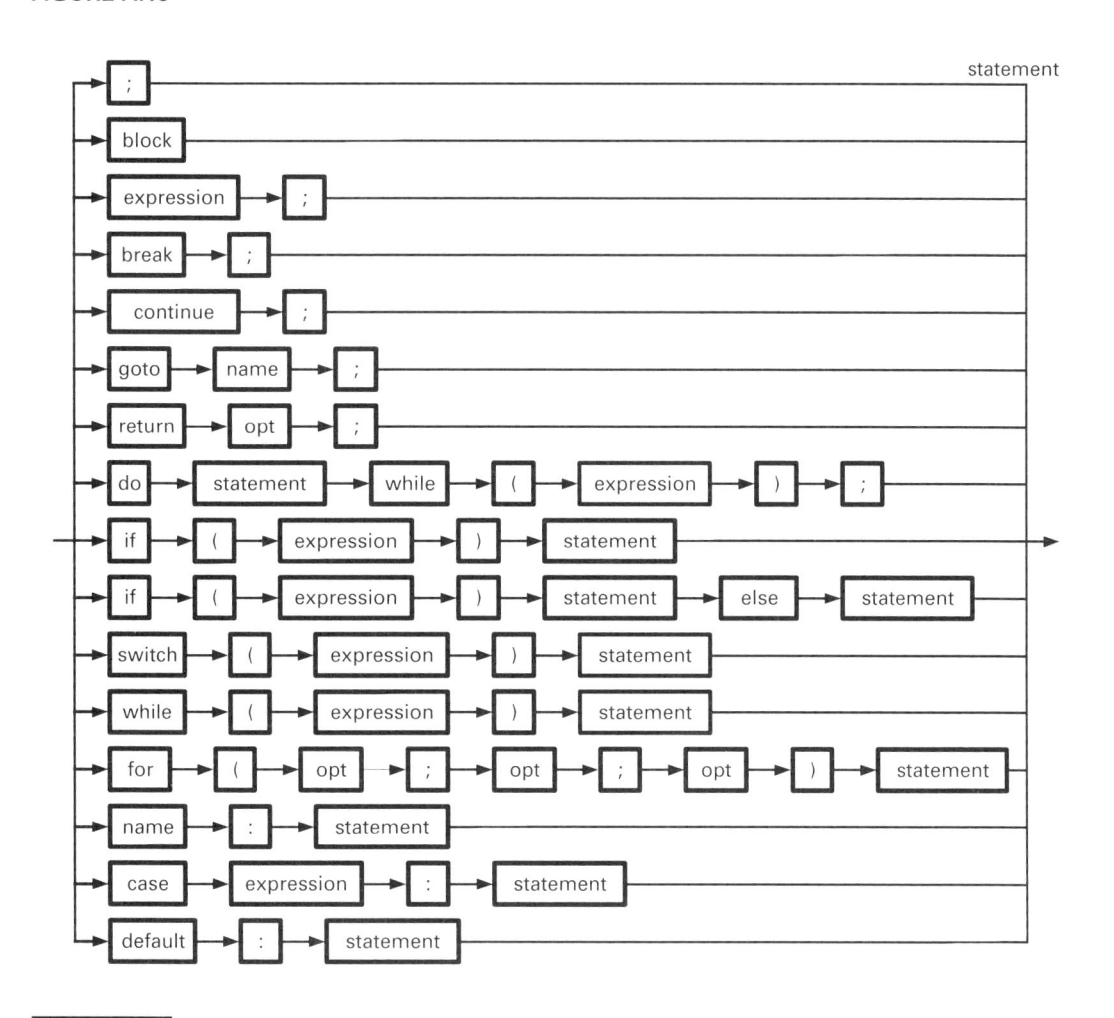

FIGURE A.15

FIGURE A.16

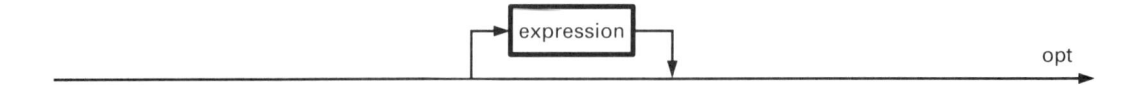

FIGURE A.17

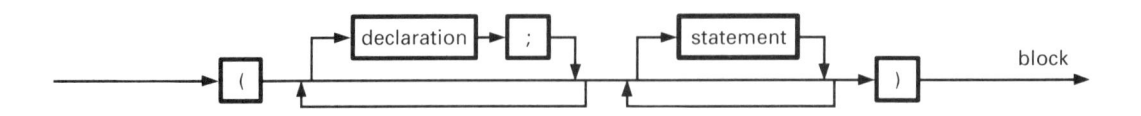

FIGURE A.18

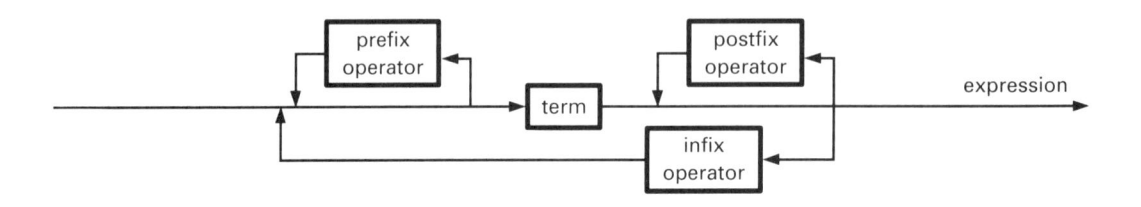

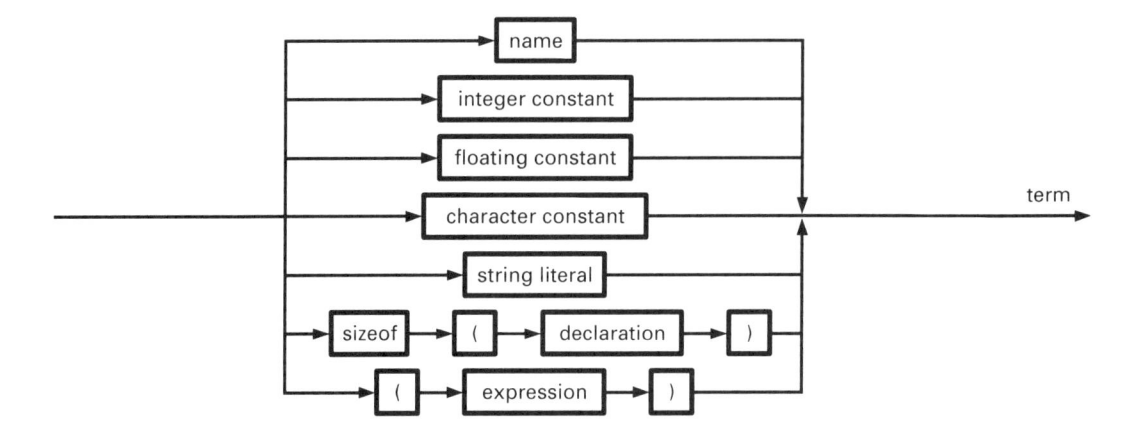

FIGURE A.19

FIGURE A.20

FUNCTION DEFINITION   **91**

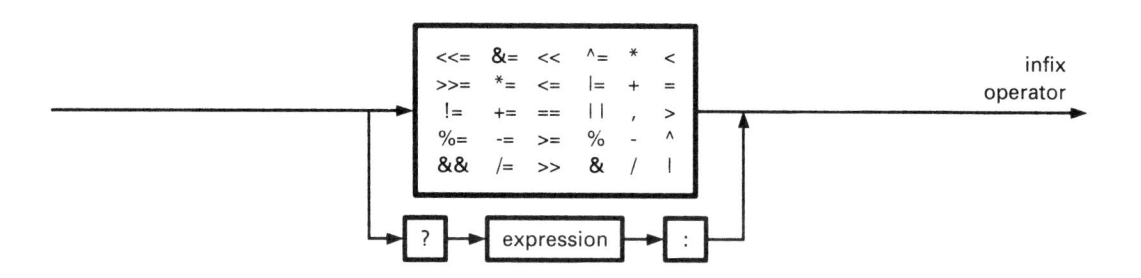

FIGURE A.21

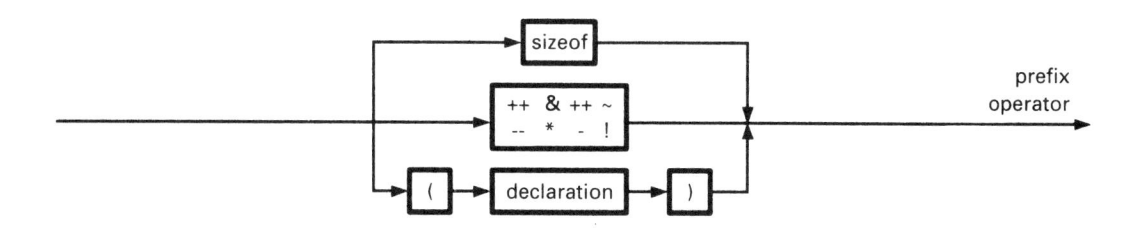

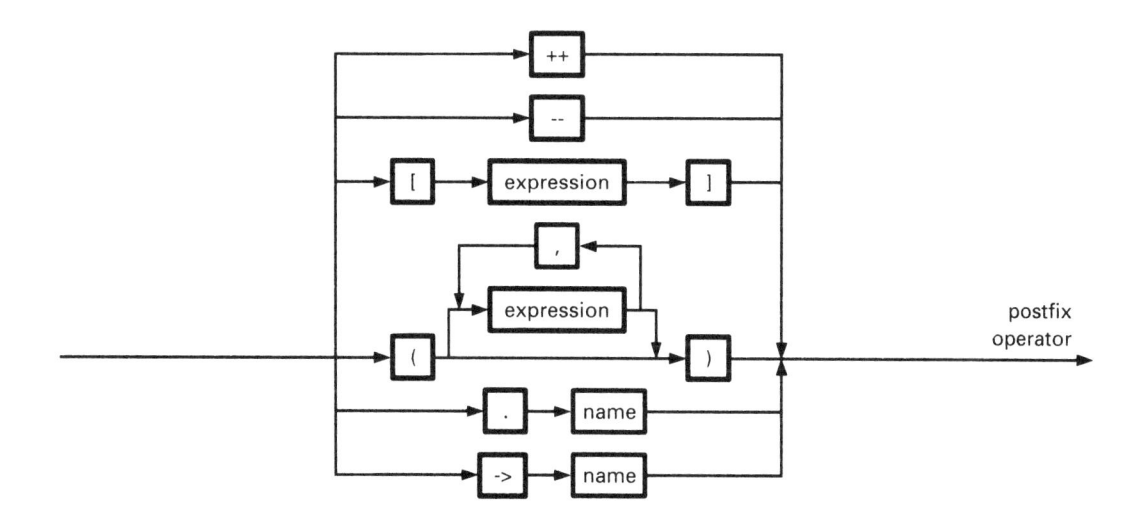

FIGURE A.22

FIGURE A.23

B

THE ASCII CHARACTER SET

This table shows the ASCII character set and its octal and hexadecimal values.

CHAR	OCT	HEX	CHAR	OCT	HEX	CHAR	OCT	HEX	CHAR	OCT	HEX
nul	0	0	sp	40	20	@	100	40	'	140	60
soh	1	1	!	41	21	A	101	41	a	141	61
stx	2	2	"	42	22	B	102	42	b	142	62
etx	3	3	'	43	23	C	103	43	c	143	63
eot	4	4	$	44	24	D	104	24	d	144	64
enq	5	5	%	45	25	E	105	45	e	145	65
ack	6	6	&	46	26	F	106	46	f	146	66
bel	7	7	'	47	27	G	107	47	g	147	67
bs	10	8	(	50	28	H	110	48	h	150	68
ht	11	9	)	51	29	I	111	49	i	151	69
nl	12	A	*	52	2A	J	112	4A	j	152	6A
vt	13	B	+	53	2B	K	113	4B	k	153	6B
np	14	C	'	54	2C	L	114	4C	l	154	6C
cr	15	D	-	55	2D	M	115	4D	m	155	6D
so	16	E	.	56	2E	N	116	4E	n	156	6E
si	17	F	/	57	2F	O	117	4F	o	157	6F
dle	20	10	0	60	30	P	120	50	p	160	70
dc1	21	11	1	61	31	Q	121	51	q	161	71
dc2	22	12	2	62	32	R	122	52	r	162	72
dc3	23	13	3	63	33	S	123	53	s	163	73

APPENDIX B THE ASCII CHARACTER SET

CHAR	OCT	HEX	CHAR	OCT	HEX	CHAR	OCT	HEX	CHAR	OCT	HEX
dc4	24	14	4	64	34	T	124	54	t	164	74
nak	25	15	5	65	35	U	125	55	u	165	75
syn	26	16	6	66	36	V	126	56	v	166	76
etb	27	17	7	67	37	W	127	57	w	167	77
can	30	18	8	70	38	X	130	58	x	170	78
em	31	19	9	71	39	Y	131	59	y	171	79
sub	32	1A	:	72	3A	Z	132	5A	z	172	7A
esc	33	1B	;	73	3B	[	133	5B	{	173	7B
fs	34	1C	<	74	3C	\	134	5C	|	174	7C
gs	35	1D	=	75	3D	]	135	5D	}	175	7D
rs	36	1E	>	76	3E	^	136	5E	~	176	7E
us	37	1F	?	77	3F	_	137	5F	del	177	7F

C

OPERATOR PRECEDENCE

This appendix lists operators in order of decreasing precedence. Operators between horizontal lines have the same precedence.

OPERATOR	DESCRIPTION
`()`	function call
`[]`	array subscripting
`->`	struct indirection
`.`	struct field selection
`++,--`	inc/dcr
`~`	one's compliment
`!`	negation
`&`	address
`*`	indirection (dereference)
`(type)`	cast
`-`	unary minus
`sizeof`	size in bytes
`*`	multiplication
`/`	division
`%`	remainder
`+`	addition
`-`	subtraction

APPENDIX C OPERATOR PRECEDENCE

OPERATOR	DESCRIPTION
<<	shift left
>>	shift right
<	less than
>	greater than
<=	less than or equal
>=	greater than or equal
==	equal
!=	not equal
&	bitwise and
^	bitwise exclusive or
|	bitwise inclusive or
&&	logical and
||	logical or
? :	conditional
= %= += -= *= /= >>= <<= &= ^= |=,	assignment
,	comma

D

C FUNCTIONS

This appendix contains short descriptions of some of the C functions. For each function we include a function prototype followed by a short description of what the function does. The standard header file containing the prototype is also given.

abs
```
#include <stdlib.h>
int abs(int integer)
```
Returns the absolute value of integer.

calloc
```
#include <stdlib.h>
char *calloc(size_t n, size_t size)
```
Allocates n*size bytes of contiguous storage and sets each byte in the storage to zero. Returns the address of the first byte allocated. If the storage cannot be allocated, calloc will return NULL.

clrscr
```
#include <conio.h> (Turbo C function)
void clrscr(void)
```
clrscr clears the current text window and places the cursor in the upper left-hand corner.

cputs
```
#include <conio.h> (Turbo C function)
int cputs(const char *str)
```
cputs writes the null-terminated string str to the current text window. It does not append a newline character. cputs returns the last character printed.

exit
```
#include <stdlib.h>
void exit(int status_value)
```
Terminates the program and sends the value status_value to the invoking process. Flushes all buffers and closes all open files.

fclose
```
#include <stdio.h>
int fclose(FILE *file_pointer)
```
Closes the file referenced by file_pointer. Flushes all buffers for this stream. If successful, fclose will return 0; otherwise it will return EOF.

feof
```
#include <stdio.h>
int feof(FILE *file_pointer)
```
Returns nonzero if end-of-file indicator was detected on the last input operation on the file referenced by file_pointer and 0 otherwise.

fgetc
```
#include <stdio.h>
int fgetc(FILE *file_pointer)
```
Returns the next character from the file that is referenced by file_pointer; or if the end of file is reached or an error occurs, it will return EOF.

fgets
```
#include <stdio.h>
char *fgets(char *storage, int max_line, FILE *file_pointer)
```
Reads the next line, which can consist of: the next max_line-1 characters, or all characters up to and including the next newline character, or all characters up to the end of the file, whichever is shortest, and stores it at the address storage. If a character is stored, fgets adds '\0' to the end of the line. If no characters are stored, fgets returns NULL, otherwise it returns the address of storage.

fopen
```
#include <stdio.h>
FILE *fopen(const char *filename, const char *mode)
```
Opens the file whose name is pointed to by filename. If mode is "a," the file will be opened for appending. If mode is "r," the file will be opened for reading. If mode is "w," the file will be opened for writing. If mode is "a+," "r+," or "w+," the file will be opened for reading and writing. fopen returns the address of a structure that allows access to the file; in case of error it returns NULL.

fprintf
```
#include<stdio.h>
int fprintf(FILE *file_pointer, const char *string, par1, par2,...)
```
Writes formatted output to the file referenced by file_pointer. The parameter string points to characters to be copied to the output as well as format specifications for the parameters par1, par2,.... fprintf returns the number of characters written, or in case of error, it returns a negative value.

fputc
```
#include <stdio.h>
int fputc(int character, FILE *file_pointer)
```
fputc writes character to the file referenced by file_pointer. fputc returns the character written, or in case of error, EOF.

fputs
```
#include <stdio.h>
int fputs(const char *string, FILE *file_pointer)
```
fputs writes string to the file referenced by file_pointer. fputs returns a nonnegative value unless an error occurs, in which case it returns EOF.

free
```
#include <stdlib.h>
void free(char *storage)
```
Frees the area beginning at storage that was previously allocated by calloc or malloc.

fscanf
```
#include <stdio.h>
int fscanf(FILE *file_pointer, const char *string, ptr1, ptr2,...)
```
Reads formatted input from the file referenced by file_pointer. The converted data are stored at addresses ptr1, ptr2,...; string contains the format specifications for the data read. If the end of file is reached before any conversion, fscanf will return EOF, otherwise, it will return the number of items read and stored.

fseek
```
#include <stdio.h>
int fseek(FILE *file_pointer, long offset, int base)
```
The file position marker for the file referenced by file_pointer is repositioned offset bytes from the beginning of the file (if base is 0), from the current position (if base is 1), or from the end of the file (if base is 2). If successful, fseek returns 0; otherwise it returns nonzero value. For text files, the offset is usually a value returned by ftell (unless offset is 0).

ftell
```
#include <stdio.h>
long ftell(FILE *file_pointer)
```
ftell returns the offset of the file position marker in bytes from the beginning of the file referenced by file_pointer.

fwrite
```
#include <stdio.h>
int fwrite(const char *storage, size_t size,
     size_t count, FILE *file_pointer)
```
Writes count items from storage, each of size bytes, to the file referenced by file_pointer.

getchar
```
#include <stdio.h>
int getchar()
```
getchar returns the next character from the standard input, or if the end of file is reached, it will return EOF.

gets
```
#include <stdio.h>
char *gets(char *storage)
```
Reads the next line from the standard input. The "next line" consists of all characters up to and including the next newline character or the end of file, whichever comes first. gets will return the address of storage where all characters except the newline are stored. It will return NULL if no characters are read.

gotoxy
```
#include <conio.h>   (Turbo C function)
void gotoxy(int x, int y)
```
gotoxy moves the cursor to the given position in the current text window. If the coordinates are in any way invalid, the call to gotoxy is ignored.

isalnum
```
#include <ctype.h>
int isalnum(int character)
```
Will return a nonzero integer if character is an alphanumeric; otherwise it will return 0.

isdigit
```
#include <ctype.h>
int isdigit(int character)
```

Will return a nonzero integer if character is a decimal digit; otherwise it will return 0.

isspace
```
#include <ctype.h>
int isspace(int character)
```

Will return a nonzero integer if character is a space character (space, tab, carriage return, formfeed, vertical tab or newline); otherwise it will return 0.

log
```
#include <math.h>
double log(double real)
```

Returns the natural logarithm of real.

log10
```
#include <math.h>
double log10(double real)
```

Returns the logarithm to the base 10 of real.

malloc
```
#include <stdlib.h>
char *malloc(size_t size)
```

Allocates size bytes of contiguous storage and the function returns the address of the first byte allocated. If the storage cannot be allocated, malloc will return NULL. Unlike calloc, malloc is not required to set each byte to 0.

memcmp
```
#include <string.h>
(In Turbo C #include<mem.h>)
   int memcmp(const void *s1, const void *s2, size_t n)
```

The function compares successive elements from two arrays of unsigned char, beginning at the addresses s1 and s2 (both of size n), until it finds elements that are not equal. If all elements are equal, the function returns zero. If the differing element from s1 is greater than the element from s2, the function returns a positive number; otherwise it returns a negative number.

memmove
```
#include <string.h>
(In Turbo C # include<mem.h>)
   void * memmove(void *s1, const void *s2, size_t n)
```

The function copies the array of char beginning at s2 to the array of char beginning at s1 (both of size n). It returns s1. memmove correctly handles the case where the two arrays overlap.

memset
```
#include <string.h>
(In Turbo C #include <mem.h>)
   void *memset(void *s, int c, size_t n)
```

The function stores (`unsigned char`) c in each of the elements of the array of `unsigned char` beginning at s, with size n. It returns s.

printf
```
#include <stdio.h>
int printf(const char *string, par1, par2,...)
```

Writes formatted output to the standard output. The parameter string points to characters to be copied to the output as well as format specifications for the parameters par1, par2,... . The function printf returns the number of characters written; in case of error, it returns EOF.

putchar
```
#include <stdio.h.
int putchar(int character)
```

Writes character to the standard output. Returns the character written, or in case of error, it returns EOF.

puts
```
#include <stdio.h>
int puts(const char *string)
```

Writes string followed by a newline to the standard output. puts does not copy the null terminator to the output; puts returns the last character written, or in case of error, it returns EOF.

scanf
```
#include <stdio.h>
int scanf(const char *string, ptr1, ptr2, ...)
```

Reads formatted input from the standard input. The converted data are stored at addresses ptr1, ptr2, ...; string contains the format specifications for data read. If the end of file is reached before any conversion, scanf will return EOF; otherwise it will return the number of items read and stored.

sprintf
```
#include <stdio.h>
int sprintf(char *storage, const char *string, par1, par2)
```

Writes formatted output to memory beginning at address storage. The parameter string points to characters to be copied to the output as well as format specifications for the parameters par1, par2,.... sprintf returns the number of characters written or, in case of error, EOF. The output is terminated by the null character.

sqrt
```
#include <math.h>
double sqrt(double real)
```
Returns the square root of real.

sscanf
```
#include <stdio.h>
int sscanf(const char *string1, const char *string2, ptr1, ptr2...)
```
Reads formatted input from string1. The converted data are stored at addresses ptr1, ptr2, ..., string2 contains the format specifications for data read. If the end of string1 is reached before any conversion, sscanf will return EOF; otherwise it will return the number of items read and stored.

strcat
```
#include <string.h>
char *strcat(char *string1, const char *string2)
```
Copies string2 to the end of string1. Returns string1 (the address of the concatenated string).

strcmp
```
#include <string.h>
int strcmp(const char *string1, const char *string2)
```
Will return a negative integer if string1 is less than string2. Will return 0 if string1 is equal to string2. Will return a positive integer if string1 is greater than string2.

strcpy
```
#include <string.h>
char *strcpy(char *string1, const char *string2)
```
Copies string2 to string1. Returns string1.

strlen
```
#include <string.h>
int strlen(const char *string)
```
Returns the length of string, the number of characters before the first null character.

strncat
```
#include <string.h>
char *strncat(char *string1, const char *string2, size_t max_len)
```
Copies string2 or max_len characters from string2, whichever is shorter, to end of string1. In either case, a terminating null is placed at the end. Returns string1.

strncmp
```
#include <string.h>
int strncmp(const char *string1, const char *string2, size_t max_len)
```

Let s denote the string obtained by choosing string2 or max_len characters from string2, whichever is shorter. Will return a negative integer if string1 is less than s. Will return 0 if string1 is equal to s. Will return a positive integer if string1 is greater than s.

strncpy
```
#include <string.h>
char *strncpy(char *string1, const char *string2, size_t max_len)
```

Copies at most max_len characters from string2 to string1. If the length of string2 is less than max_len, then string1 is padded with null characters. The resulting string will not be null terminated if the length of string2 is greater than or equal to max_len. Returns string1.

tolower
```
#include <ctype.h>
int tolower(int character)
```

Converts character from uppercase to lowercase and returns the converted value. If character is not 'A' through 'Z,' tolower will simply return character.

toupper
```
#include <ctype.h>
int toupper(int character)
```

Converts character from lowercase to uppercase and returns the converted value. If character is not 'a' through 'z,' toupper will simply return character.

wherex
```
#include <conio.h>  (Turbo C function)
int wherex(void)
```

Returns the x-coordinate of the current cursor position (within the current text window).

wherey
```
#include <conio.h>  (Turbo C function)
int wherey(void)
```

Returns the y-coordinate of the current cursor position (within the current text window).

E

TURBO C HOT KEYS

No matter where you are in the Turbo C environment, when a hot key is pressed, its specific function is carried out. The only exception is when presented with a dialog box. (The following table is reprinted with permission from [Turbo C88U].)

KEY(S)	FUNCTION
F1	Brings up a Help window with information about your current position
F2	Saves the file currently in the Editor
F3	Lets you load a file (an input box will appear)
F4	Runs program to line the cursor is on
F5	Zooms and unzooms the active window
F6	Switches active windows
F7	Runs program in debug mode
F8	Runs program in debug mode
F9	Performs a "make"
F10	Toggles between the menus and the active window
Ctrl-F1	Calls up context help on functions (TC Editor only)
Ctrl-F2	Resets running program
Ctrl-F3	Brings up call stack
Ctrl-F4	Evaluates an expression
Ctrl-F7	Adds a watch expression
Ctrl-F8	Toggles breakpoints On and Off
Ctrl-F9	Runs program
Shift-F10	Displays the version screen

APPENDIX E TURBO C HOT KEYS

KEY(S)	FUNCTION
Alt-F1	Brings up the last help screen you referenced
Alt-F3	Lets up pick a file to load
Alt-F5	Switches between main TC screen and User screen
Alt-F6	Switches contents of active window
Alt-F7	Takes you to previous error
Alt-F8	Takes you to next error
Alt-F9	Compiles to .OBJ the file loaded in the TC Editor
Alt-B	Takes you to the Break/Watch menu
Alt-C	Takes you to the Compile menu
Alt-D	Takes you to the Debug menu
Alt-E	Puts you in the Editor
Alt-F	Takes you to the File menu
Alt-O	Takes you to the Options menu
Alt-P	Takes you to the Project menu
Alt-R	Takes you to the Run menu
Alt-X	Quits TC and returns you to DOS

F

SOLUTIONS TO CHAPTER EXERCISES

CHAPTER 2

1.  ```
    /*program to compute the number of minutes, hours,
      and days in a given number of seconds.*/

    main()
    /*program to compute the number of minutes, hours and days
     *in a given number of seconds.*/
    {
      long int sec,min,hr,day;

      printf("Enter number of seconds.\n");
      scanf("%ld", &sec);
      min = sec / 60;
      hr = min  / 60;
      day = hr / 24;
      printf("The # min = %ld, hr = %ld, day = %ld",min,hr,day);
      printf(" in %ld seconds\n", sec);
    }
    ```

2. int, 1st, _ of_items, value_in_$

3. n = 69, n = 105, n = 45

4. a = 35, b = 280, c = 287, d = 280

5. -1
   4
   0
   -2
   0

107
    ```

```
16
0, 2, 2
1, 2, 2
```

CHAPTER 3

1. ```
   largest = (a > b) ? a : b;
   ```

2. ```
   /*program to use nested if to sort 3 integers in ascending
     *order*/
   main()
   {
     int p,q,r,temp ;
     printf("Enter three integers.\n");
     scanf("%d%d%d", &p, &q, &r);
     if ( q < p || r < p)
        if( q < r)
        {           /*swap p and q*/
           temp = q;
           q = p;
           p = temp;
        }
        else
        {           /*swap p and r*/
           temp = r;
           r  = p;
           p = temp;
        }
      if( r < q )
         {
         temp = r; /*swap r and q*/
          r = q;
          q = temp;
         }
      printf("Numbers in ascending order:%d, %d, %d,\n", p,q,r);
   }
   ```

3. ```
   /*Program to display digits in English*/
   main()
   {
      int digit;
      printf("Enter a single digit.\n");
      scanf("%d", &digit);
      switch (digit)
      {
       case 0: printf("ZERO\n"); break;
       case 1: printf("ONE\n"); break;
       case 2: printf("TWO\n"); break;
       case 3: printf("THREE\n"); break;
   ```
   ```

```
           case 4: printf("FOUR\n"); break;
           case 5: printf("FIVE\n"); break;
           case 7: printf("SEVEN\n"); break;
           case 8: printf("EGIHT\n"); break;
           case 9: printf("NINE\n"); break;
           default: printf("Illegal input\n");
             }
       }
```

4. ```
   /*Program to print out a five-row equilateral triangle of
   stars.*/
   main()

   {
       int i = 1, k = 0, j;
       for ( ; i <= 5; ++i, k++)
       {       for (j = 1; j <= 5-i; j++)
                 printf(" ");
               for (j = 1; j <= i + k; j++)
                 printf("*"); /*print i stars*/
               printf("\n");       /*return to next line*/
       }
   }
   ```

5. ```
   /*Program to reverse the digits of a positive integer*/
   main()
   {
       unsigned digit, number, reverse = 0;
       printf("Enter a positive integer.\n");
       scanf("%d", &number);
       while (number > 0)
       {
           digit = number % 10;
           number = number /10;
           reverse = 10 * reverse + digit;
        }
        printf("The reverse of %d is %d\n",number,reverse);
   }
   ```

6. 1 ,0, 3
   5 ,10
   4 ,5

CHAPTER 4

1. ```
   /*Program to reverse the entries of a 5 floating
   *point array, first by using indices and second by
   *using pointers.*/
   main()
   {
   ```
   ```

```
    float numbers[] ={2.5,3,-7.3,9,0}, temp, *p, *q;
    int i;
    for (i =0; i< 5; i++)/*print array*/
       printf("% 6.2f",numbers[i]);
    printf("\n");
    for(i=0; i<5/2; i++)   /* reverse using indices*/
    {
        temp = numbers[i];
        numbers[i] = numbers[4-i];
        numbers[4-i] = temp;
    }
    for (i =0; i< 5; i++)
        printf("% 6.2f",numbers[i]);
    printf("\n");
    for (p = numbers, q = numbers+4; p < q; p++, q--)
    {
        temp = *p;
        *p = *q;
        *q = temp;
    }
    for (p = numbers; p <= numbers + 4; p++)
        printf("% 6.2f", *p);
    printf("\n");
    }
```

2.
```
    /* Program to compare two inputed strings and determine
     * if they are identical. */

    main()
    {
      int i;
      char string1[15],string2[15];
      printf("Enter a stirng of characters.\n");
      scanf("%s",string1);
      printf("Enter another string of characters.\n");
      scanf("%s",string2);
      if ( strlen(string1) == strlen(string2) )
         for (i=0; i< strlen(string1); i++)
            if( string1[i] != string2[i] )
               break;
      if( strlen(string1) != strlen(string2) ||
          i != strlen(string1) )
          printf("The two strings are not identical.\n");
      else
          printf("The two strings are identical.\n");
    }
```

3. ```
/*Program to determine if tomorrow is a weekend or a week day,
 given the day of the week today./
main()
{
    enum days
    {sunday, monday, tuesday, wednesday, thursday, friday,
        saturday} day;
    int i;

    printf("Enter the day of the week .\n");
    printf("type 0 for sun. 1 for mon. ...\n");
    scanf("%d", &i);
    if ((enum days) (i) == friday)
        printf("Tomorrow is a weekend day.\n");
     else
        printf("Tomorrow is a week day.\n");
}
```

4. ```
main()
{
    struct time
    {
        int hour;
        int minutes;
        int seconds;

    } a_time,time_passed, new_time;
    int temp;

    printf("Enter a given time. \n");
    scanf("%d%d%d",&a_time.hour, &a_time.minutes,
          &a_time.seconds);
    printf("Enter a given time passed. \n");
    scanf("%d%d%d",&time_passed.hour, &time_passed.minutes,
          &time_passed.seconds);
    printf("The new time will be :\n");
    new_time.seconds = (a_time.seconds + time_passed.seconds) % 60;
    temp =(a_time.seconds + time_passed.seconds) / 60;
    new_time.minutes = (a_time.minutes +
                        time_passed.minnutes + temp) % 60;
    temp = (a_time.minutes + time_passed.minutes + temp) / 60;
    new_time.hour =(a_time.hour + time_passed.hour + temp) % 60;
    printf("%d : %d: %d \n",new_time.hour,
          new_time.minutes, new_time.seconds);
}
```

5.
```c
/*Program to compute the total number of credits earned
  *by a given number of students and to compute the
  *average of their GPA*/
#include <stdio.h>
#define MAX_STUDENTS 30 /*MAX_STUDENTS is a constant for the
             *maximum number of students*/
main()
{
    float average = 0.0;
    int j = 0,i,n = 0;
    struct student
    {
      char name [15];
             /*There are at most 15 characters in a name*/
        int credits;
        float GPA;
        char gender;
    };
     struct student class[MAX_STUDENTS];
                       /*class is an array of students*/
    float total_GPA = 0;
    printf("Enter the average GPA.\n");
    scanf("%f",&average);
    printf("The school average GPA is %f\n", average);
    printf("Enter the number of students.\n");
    scanf("%d",&n);
    for (i = 0; i < n; ++i)
    {
    printf("Enter a student name.\n");
        scanf("%15s", class[i].name);
        printf("Enter student's credits GPA and sex.\n");
        scanf("%d%f %c",&class[i].credits,&class[i].GPA,
                 &class[i].gender);
    total_GPA += class[i].gender;
    j += class[i].credits;
    }
     printf("    name      credits   GPA  sex\n");
     for( i = 0; i < n; ++i)
     {
     printf("%-15s     %3d    ",
            class[i].name,class[i].credits);
     printf("%5.2f   %c\n",class[i].GPA,class[i].gender);
     }
     printf("The total number of credits earned: %d\n",j);
     printf("The grade point average is: %5.2f\n",
            total_GPA/n);
}
```

6. 2345
   1 ,1 ,1
   1
   2 ,1

CHAPTER 5

1.
```c
/* function to return a raised to the power b*/
     long int a_to_the_b(int a,int b);
main()
{
    int a,b;

    printf("Enter two integers a and b.\n");
    scanf("%d%d",&a,&b);
    printf("%d to the power %d is %ld\n",a,b,a_to_the_b(a,b));
}

long int a_to_the_b(int a,int b)
{
    int i;
    longint result = 1;

    if ( b == 0)
        return(1);
    else
    {
    for (i = 0 ; i < b; i++)
        result *=a;
    return(result)
    }
}
```

2.
```c
/* Two functions adding 3X4 matrices.
 * One with three arguments, and one
 * with two arguments.*/

int  c[3][4];
void add(int a[3][],int b[3][],int c[3][]);
void add_glob(int a[3][4],int b[3][4]);
void print(int a[3][4]);

main()
{
    int  a[3][4] = { {2,6,-1,5},
              {5,0,2,-9},
              {8,-4,6,8} };
    int  b[3][4] = { {3,5,7,-2},
              {-5, 6,0,0},
              {3,6,-2,9} };
    print(a);
    printf(" +\n");
    print(b);
    add(a,b,c);
    print(c);
    add_glob(a,b);
    print(c);
```

```
}
void print(int a[3][4])
{
int i,j;

for (i = 0; i < 3 ; i++)
    {
    for(j = 0; j < 4; j++)
        printf("%4d",a[i][j]);
     printf("\n");     }
     }
     printf("\n");
}

void add(int a[3][4],int b[3][4],int c[3][4])
{
    int i,j;
    for(i = 0; i < 3 ; i++)
        for( j = 0; j < 4; j++)
            c[i][j] = a[i][j] + b[i][j];
}
void add_glob(int a[3][4],int b[3][4])
{
    int i,j;
    for(i = 0; i < 3 ; i++)
        for( j = 0; j < 4; j++)
            c[i][j] = a[i][j] + b[i][j];
}
```

3.
```
/* program to test a character string to
 * see if it is a palindrome.*/

main()
{
   char string[15];
   int is_palindrome(char string[]);

   printf("Enter a string to be tested.\n");
   scanf("%s",string);
   if (is_palindrome(string))
     printf("The string %s is a palindrome.\n",string);
   else
     printf("The string %s is not a palindrome.\n",string);
}
int is_palindrome(char string[])
{
   int palind = 1;
   char *fptr = string ,*rptr = &string[strlen(string) -1];
```

```
          while( fptr < rptr)
           {
            if( *fptr != *rptr)
            palind = 0;
            fptr++;
            rptr--;
           }
           return(palind);
        }
```

4. `/*function to count the number of words in a line of text*/`

```
   char string[] = "Working with C strings is fun.";
   int count(char *string);
   main()
   {
        printf("There are %d words in %s\n",
               count(string),string);
   }
   int count(char *string)
   {

   int count(char *string)
        int i = 0, j = 0;
        while( string[j] != '\0')
        {
             if(string[j] == ' ')
                  i++;
             j++;
        }
        return(i+1);
   }
```

5. `/*functions to swap, print and sort an array`
   `*in descending order*/`

```
   int numbers[] = { 3,5,-4,7,0,-5,1,6,34,5};
   int n = 10;
   int max();
   void sort();
   void swap(int *a_pointer, int *b_pointer);
   void print_nums();

   main()
   {
      print_nums();
      printf("\nThe largest number is = %d\n",max());
      sort();
      printf("After sorting,");
      print_nums();
```

```
      }
      int max()
      {
        int i,largest;

        largest = numbers[0];
        for ( i = 1; i < n; i++)
          if(numbers[i] > largest)
             largest = numbers[i];
        return(largest);
      }
      void sort()
      {
         int i,j;
         for ( i = 0; i < n-1; i++)
           for (j = i + 1; j < n; j++)
           if(numbers[i] < numbers[j])
              swap(&numbers[i], &numbers[j]);
      }

      void swap(int *a_pointer, int *b_pointer)
      {
        int temp;

        temp = *a_pointer;
        *a_pointer = *b_pointer;
        *b_pointer = temp;
      }
      void print_nums()
      {
        int i;
        printf("The numbers are:\n");
        for ( i = 0; i < n; i++)
          printf("%5d",numbers[i]);
      }
```

6. 1
   2
   4
   1

CHAPTER 6

Exercises 1–4

The following program uses arguments on the command line to perform the task of counting the number of characters or the number of lines or the number of words in a file.

```c
/*Usage:
 *count filename character | word | line.
 *This program counts the number or characters or
 *words or lines in the file whose name is the
 *first command line argument.*/
#include <stdio.h>
int char_count(FILE *fp);
int word_count(FILE *fp);
int line_count(FILE *fp);

int char_count(FILE *fp)
{
   char ch_count = 0;
   while( getc(fp) != EOF )
     ch_count++;
   return(ch_count);
}

int word_count(FILE *fp)
{
   char word[20];
   int wrd_count = 0;
   while( fscanf(fp,"%s",word) != EOF )
     wrd_count++;
   return(wrd_count);
}

int line_count(FILE *fp)
{
  char line[100];
  int ln_count = 0;
  while ( fgets(line,100,fp) != NULL)
    ln_count++;
  return(ln_count);
}

main(int argc,char *argv[])
{
   int i;
   FILE *fp;

   for (i = 2; i < argc; i++)
   {
   printf("argv[%d] = %s\n",i,argv[i]);
       fp = fopen( argv[1], "r");
       if( strcmp(argv[i],"character") == 0)
          printf("There are %d characters in file %s.\n",
              char_count(fp),argv[1]);
       else if( strcmp(argv[i],"word") == 0)
          printf("There are %d words in file %s.\n",
              word_count(fp),argv[1]);
          else  if( strcmp(argv[i], "line") == 0)
              printf("There are %d lines in file %s.\n",
```

```
                         line_count(fp),argv[1]);
            fclose(fp);
        }
}
Program Input (data)

This is a test file
to count the number of
characters, words, and lines.

command line

count data character word line

Program Output

argv[2] = character
There are 72 characters in file data.
argv[3] = word
There are 14 words in file data.
argv[4] = line
There are 3 lines in file data.
```

CHAPTER 7

Exercises 1–4

```
/*Program to create a link list of times of the day,
 *to insert and delete nodes and to print the list.*/

#include <stdlib.h>
#include <stdio.h>

typedef struct node *NODEPTR;
struct node
   {
    char AM_PM;
    int hour;
    int min;
    NODEPTR next;
   };
struct node time,time1,time2,time3;
NODEPTR head;

NODEPTR make_list();
NODEPTR find_location(struct node time, NODEPTR head);
int insert_after(NODEPTR prev, struct node time);
void delete(NODEPTR p,struct node time);
void print(NODEPTR head);
```

```
NODEPTR make_list()
/*function to create a list with the time 0:0 AM*/
{
      head = (NODEPTR) malloc(sizeof(struct node));
      head->AM_PM = 'a';
      head->hour = 0;
      head->min = 0;
      head->next = NULL;
      return (head);
}

int insert_after(NODEPTR head, struct node time)
/* function to insert a node after the node pointed to
   by prev.  Return 0 if malloc fails, 1 otherwise.*/
{
   NODEPTR new,prev;

   prev = find_location(time,head);
   if( (new = (NODEPTR) malloc(sizeof(struct node))) != 0)
    {
      new -> AM_PM = time.AM_PM;
       new -> hour = time. hour;
       new -> min = time.min;
       new -> next = prev->next;
       prev -> next = new;
    }
   return( new != NULL );
}

NODEPTR find_location(struct node time, NODEPTR head)
/*function to return a pointer to a node after which
 *the node time is to be inserted*/
{
      NODEPTR p = head;
      if (time.AM_PM == 'p')
           while( p->next != NULL && p->next->AM_PM == 'a')
            p = p->next;
      while (p->next != NULL && p->next->AM_PM == time.AM_PM &&
             p->next->hour < time.hour)
           p = p->next;
      while (p->next != NULL && p->next->AM_PM == time.AM_PM &&
              p->next->hour == time.hour && p->next->min < time.min)
           p = p->next;
       return(p);
}

void print_list(NODEPTR l)
{
  for(;l != NULL; l = l->next)
    printf("%5d:%02d %cm\n", l->hour, l->min, l->AM_PM);
  printf("*******************\n");
}
```

```
void delete(NODEPTR head, struct node time)
/*function to delete time from the list head.*/
{
      NODEPTR p;

      p =find_location(time,head);
      if( (p->next->AM_PM == time.AM_PM) &&
           (p->next->hour == time.hour) &&
           (p->next->min == time.min) )
             p->next = (p->next)->next;
      else
             printf("Can not delete.\n");
 }
main()
{
      NODEPTR p;

      head = make_list();
      time1.AM_PM = 'p'; time1.hour = 3; time.min = 26;
      time2.AM_PM = 'a'; time2.hour = 11; time2.min = 5;
      time3.AM_PM = 'a'; time3.hour = 6; time3.min = 9;
      print_list (head);
      insert_after(head,time1);
      insert_after(head,time2);
      insert_after(head,time3);
      print_list (head);
      delete(head,time2);
      print_list(head);
      delete(p,time2);
      print_list(head);
}
```

5.
```
/*function to print the data in a node of a binary tree
*together with the node's number of descendants*/

int descendant(NODEPTR root)
{
      int count = 0;
      if (root == NULL)
           return(0);
      if(root->left != NULL)
           count += 1 + descendant(root->left);
      if(root->right != NULL)
           count += 1 + descendant(root->right);
      printf("Node %d has %d descendants.\n",
           root->data, count);
      return(count);
}
```

CHAPTER 8

1. ```
#define MAX(a,b) ((a) > (b) ? (a) : (b))
```

2. ```
#define IS_DIGIT(c) (  ('0' <= c  &&  c <= '9') ? 1 : 0)
```

3. ```
#define SWAP(type,a,b) \
              { type temp = (a); (a) = (b); (b) = temp;}
   int c, d;
   float r, s;
      ...
   SWAP(int,c ,d);
   SWAP(float, r,s);
```

# CHAPTER 9

1. ```
main()
{
int a[4][3] = { {7, 3, 0},
         {5, 3, 7},
           {-1, 6, 0},
           {9, 4, 6} };
int b[3][2] = { {8, 3},
         {4, 0},
         {2, 5} };
int c[4][2],i,j,k;

  for(i =0; i<4 ; i++)
    for(j =0; j< 2; j++)
    {
       c[i][j] =0;
       for(k = 0; k < 3; k++)
 c[i][j] += a[i][k]*b[k][j];
     }

  for(i = 0; i < 4; i++)
  {
    for(j = 0; j < 2; j ++)
      printf("%4d",c[i][j]);
      printf("\n");
   }

}
```

2. ```c
/*Program to open a window and display in it the content of a
file.
  If the content of the file does not fit into the window, the
  user is instructed to press enter before the rest of the file
  is displayed.*/

#include <conio.h>
#include <stdio.h>

main(argc, argv)
int argc;
char *argv[];
{
    FILE *fp;
    char ch[81];
    int line;

    if (argc == 1) /* arg[1] is the command line argument
                   which is the name of the file to
                   be displayed.*/
     {
        fprintf(stderr,"Usage: prog3 <filename>\n");
        exit(1);
     }

     clrscr();
     gotoxy(15,16);
     printf("file name: %s", argv[1]);
     window(15,8,50,20); /*top left of window is (15,8)
                   bottom right is (50,20)*/
    if ((fp = fopen(argv[1],"r")) == NULL)
    {
        fprintf(stderr,"Could not open file %s\n", argv[1]);
        exit(1);
    }

    for (line = 1; fgets(ch,37,fp) != NULL; ++line)
    {
        if (line % 12 == 0) /*if at end of window*/
        {
            gotoxy(20,12);
            cputs("Press Enter ...");
            getch();
            clrscr();
        }
        cputs(ch);
        putch('\r');
    }
}
```
```

CHAPTER 10

1.
```cpp
// array.h - Definition of class array for chapter 10
// A variable of type 'class array' is an ordinary C array with
// bounds checking and additional operations, such as
// comparison.

#include <stdlib.h>

class array {
  private:
     unsigned nbr_elements;  // current length of array
     unsigned max_size;      // room for max_size elements
     int *elements; // the array itself

     array & init(unsigned initial_size, unsigned size = 1);

 protected:
     // insert and remove (an array member) can only be
     // used by derived classes:
     array & insert(unsigned i, int member);
     array & remove(unsigned i);

     // change the nbr of elements; realloc if necessary:
     array & resize(unsigned new_size);

     array & make_empty() {  // remove all elements
         nbr_elements = 0;
         return *this;
     }

     int & quit(unsigned i) const;  //see operator []

  public:
     // create an empty array :
     array(unsigned max_size=1) { init(max_size); }

     array(const array &);  // copy constructor

     ~array() {  // destroy an array
         free(elements);
     }

     unsigned size() const { return nbr_elements; }

     array & operator = (const array &);

     int & operator [](unsigned i) const {
         return i >= nbr_elements ? quit(i) : elements[i];
     }
```

```
        // compare two arrays:
        int operator == (const array &) const;
        int operator != (const array &a) const {
            return ! operator == (a);
        }

        virtual void print();
};

// array.cpp - Definition of member functions for class array

#include <stdio.h>
#include <stdlib.h>
#include <stdarg.h>
#if defined __TURBOC__
#include <mem.h>
#endif

#include "array.h"

#define TRUE 1
#define FALSE 0

// allocate memory for member 'elements':
array & array::init(unsigned initial_size, unsigned size)
{
    nbr_elements = initial_size;
    max_size = (size > nbr_elements) ? size :
                  (initial_size > 0) ? initial_size : 1;
    elements = (int *)calloc(max_size, sizeof(int));
       return *this;
       }

// copy constructor:
array::array(const array & a) {
      init(a.nbr_elements,a.max_size);
      memcpy(elements, a.elements, max_size * sizeof(int));
}

// if a1 and a2 are arrays, then for the assignment a1 = a2,
// we need to make a copy of the 'elements' array:
array & array::operator = (const array &a)
{
  if (*this == a)
     return *this;

if (max_size < a.max_size)
     resize(a.max_size);   // make a bigger array
  nbr_elements = a.size();
```

```
    if (size() > 0)
        memcpy(elements, a.elements, size() * sizeof(int));
    return *this;
    }

// compare the equality of two arrays:
int array::operator == (const array &a) const
{
    unsigned i;

    if (nbr_elements != a.nbr_elements)
        return FALSE;

    for (i = 0; i < nbr_elements; ++i) {
        if ((*this)[i] != a[i])
            return FALSE;
        }

    return TRUE;
    }

// change the size of the array;
// if the current array can hold fewer than 'new_size' elements,
// then we must allocate new memory for the array.
// the amount of allocated memory is never shrunk
array & array::resize(unsigned new_size)
{
    nbr_elements = new_size;
    if (new_size > max_size) {
        max_size = new_size;
        elements = (int *)realloc(elements, max_size *
                    sizeof(int));
        }
    return *this;
    }

// insert a new element at position 'i'; if necessary, shift the
// following elements to make room:
array & array::insert(unsigned i, int member)
{
    unsigned oldsize = size ();

    resize(i < oldsize ? oldsize+1 : i+1);

    if (i < oldsize ? oldsize+1 : i+1);
        memmove(&elements[i+1], &elements[i], (oldsize-i)*sizeof(int));

    (*this)[i] = member;
    return *this;
    }
```

```cpp
// remove an element;  if it is not the last, shift the
// remaining elements to close the gap:
array & array::remove(unsigned i)
{

    if (i < nbr_elements) {
        if (i < --nbr_elements)   /* Not deleting last element */
          memmove(&elements[i], &elements[i+1],
                  (nbr_elements-i)*sizeof(int));
        }
    return *this;
    }

// print the elements of the array separated by commas.
void array::print()
{
    unsigned i;

    for (i = 0; i < size(); ++i) {
        if (i > 0) {
            putchar(','); putchar(' ');
            }
        printf("%d", (*this)[i]);
        }
    return;
    }

int & array::quit(unsigned i) const {
    fprintf(stderr, "Index %d greater than %d.\n", i,
nbr_elements-1);
    exit(EXIT_FAILURE);
    return elements[0];
    }

// set.h - Definition of class set for chapter 10
// A set is an unordered list of elements
// The usual set operations (union, intersection, and difference)
// are defined.  In addition two sets may be compared for equality
// or to determine if one is a subset of the other.

#include "array.h"   //a set will be implemented as an array

class set : public array {
 private:
    //cast an array to a set (simplifies binary operations):
    set (const array &a) : array(a) {}

    // find the position of 'e'.
    // Return TRUE if 'e' is an element of the set.
    int find_element(int e, unsigned &i) const;
```

```cpp
public:
    // create an empty set with room for 'size' elements;
    set(unsigned size=1) : array(size) { make_empty();}

    set(const set &s) : array(s) {} //copy constructor

    // create a set with one or more elements:
    set(unsigned count, int element, ...);

    // add 'count' elements to the set:
    set & add_elements(unsigned count, int element, ...);

    // return TRUE/FALSE if e is/is not in the set
    int is_element(int e) const {
        unsigned dummy;
        return find_element(e, dummy);
      }

    //  redefine operator [] so that, for example,
    //  s[i] = 3 is not possible:
    int operator [] (unsigned i) const {
        return array::operator [] (i);
          }

    set operator | (const set &s) const;  // set union
    set & operator |= (const set &s);

    set operator & (const set &s) const;  // intersection
    set & operator &= (const set &s);

    set operator - (const set &s) const;  // set difference
    set & operator -= (const set &s);

    int operator <= (const set &s) const;  // is a subset

    int operator >= (const set &s) const {  // is a superset
        return s.operator <= (*this);
    }

    int is_empty() const { return size() == 0; }
    set & make_empty() {
        array::make_empty();
        return *this;
        }

        void print();
};
```

```cpp
// set.cpp - Definition of member functions for class set

#include <stdio.h>
#include <stdarg.h>
#include "set.h"

#define TRUE 1
#define FALSE 0

// locate 'e' in the set; on return 'i' is the
// position of 'e' in the set (or the position it would
// occupy if added to the set).
// Returns TRUE/FALSE if 'e' is/is not in the set
int set::find_element(int e, unsigned &i) const
{
    for (i = size(); i > 0; --i)
        if (e > (*this)[i-1])
            break;
    return i < size() && e == (*this)[i];
     }

// create a set with one or more elements:
set::set(unsigned count, int first, ...) : array(count)
{
    va_list ap;
    unsigned i, unsigned i,j;
    int element = first;

    make_empty();   // no elements to start (makes insertions easier)
    if (count > 0) {
        va_start(ap, first);
        for (i = 0; i < count; ++i) {
            if ( ! find_element(element, j)) {
                insert(j, element);
                }
            element = va_arg(ap, int);
            }
        }
    va_end(ap);
    }

// add 'count' elements to the set:
set & set::add_elements(unsigned count, int first, ...)
{
    va_list ap;
    unsigned i, j;
    int element = first;
    unsigned oldsize = size();

    if (count == 0)
        return *this;
```

```
    resize(oldsize+count);
    resize(oldsize);          // backup to old size
    va_start(ap, first);
    for (i = 0; i < count; ++i) {
        if ( ! find_element(element, j))
            insert(j, element);
        element = va_arg(ap, int);
        }
     va_end(ap);
     return *this;
     }

//compute the union of two sets:
set set::operator | (const set &s) const
{
    unsigned i, j, k;
    unsigned count;

    // compute how many elements are in the union:
    i = j = count = 0;
    while (i < size() && j < s.size()) {
        ++count;
        if ((*this)[i] == s[j]) {
            ++i; ++j;
            }
        else if ((*this)[i] < s[j])
            ++i;
        else
            ++j;
        }

    count += (size() - i) + (s.size() - j);

    array temp(count);

    // merge the elements of the two sets into 'temp':
    for (i = j = k = 0; i < size() && j < s.size(); ++k) {
        if ((*this)[i] <= s[j]) {
         temp[k] = (*this)[i];
         if ((*this)[i++] == s[j])
              ++j;
         }
        else
            temp[k] = s[j++];
        }

    while (i < size())
        temp[k++] = (*this)[i++];
    while (j < s.size())
        temp[k++] = s[j++];
```

```
        return temp;
    }

// compute the intersection of two sets:
set set::operator & (const set &s) const
{

    unsigned i, j, k;
    // 'temp' will hold the elements in the intersection:
    array temp(size() < s.size() ? size() : s.size());

    i = j = k = 0;
    while (i < size() && j < s.size()) {
        if ((*this)[i] == s[j]) { //found an element in the intersection
            temp[k] = s[j];
            ++i, ++k, ++j;
            }
        else if ((*this)[i] < s[j])
            ++i;
        else
            ++j;
        }
    set s_temp(temp);
    s_temp.resize(k);
    return s_temp;
    }

// set difference; e.g. after a = b - c, a contains the
// elements in b and not in c
set set::operator - (const set &s) const
{

    array temp(size());
    unsigned i, j, k;

    i = j = k = 0;
    while (i < size() && j < s.size()) {
        if ((*this)[i] == s[j]) {
            ++i; ++j;
            }
        else if ((*this)[i] < s[j])
            temp[k++] = (*this)[i++];
        else
            ++j;
        }
    while (i < size())
        temp[k++] = (*this)[i++];

    set s_temp(temp);
    s_temp.resize(k);
    return s_temp;
    }
```

```
// boolean: a <= b is TRUE if a is a subset of b
int set::operator <= (const set &s) const
{

    unsigned i, j;
    i = j = 0;
    unsigned s1 = size(), s2 = s.size();

    if (s1 == 0)
        return TRUE;
    if (s1 > s2 || (*this)[s1-1] > s[s2-1])
        return FALSE;
    // at this point 0 < s1 <= s2 and the largest element of *this
    // is <= the largest element of 's'.
    while (i < s1) {
        if ( (*this)[i] == s[j]) {
            ++i, ++j;
            }
        else if ((*this)[i] < s[j])
            return FALSE;
        else
            ++j;
        }

    return TRUE;
    }

// a |= b replaces a with the union of a and b:
set & set::operator |= (const set &s)
{

    unsigned i, j;

    for (i = j = 0; i < size() && j < s.size(); ++i) {
        if ((*this)[i] == s[j]) {
            ++j;
            }
        else if ((*this)[i] > s[j])
            insert(i, s[j++]);
        }

    while (j < s.size() )
        insert(i++, s[j++]);

    return *this;
     }

// a &= b replaces a with the intersection of a and b:
set & set::operator &= (const set &s)
{
    unsigned i, j;
    i = j = 0;
    while (i < size() && j < s.size()) {
```

```
                if ((*this)[i] == s[j]) {
                    ++i, ++j;
                }
                else if ((*this)[i] < s[j])
                 remove(i);
                else
                    ++j;
            }
        resize(i);
        return *this;
        }

set & set::operator -= (const set &s) //a -= b replaces a with a-b;
{

    unsigned i, j;

    i = j = 0;
    while (i < size() && j < s.size()) {
        if ((*this)[i] == s[j]) {
            remove(i); ++j;
            }
        else if ((*this)[i] < s[j])
            ++i;
        else
            ++j;
            }

    return *this;
    }

void set::print()
{

    putchar ('{');
    array::print();
    putchar('}');
    return;
        }

// test10-1.cpp - Program to test class set

#include <stdio.h>
#include "set.h"

#define print_set(s)   printf(#s " = "); (s).print(); putchar('\n');

main()
{
```

```
    set a(12,27,-17,23,4,50,6,100,-451,19,36,101,1);
    set b(12);
    set c(30),d(30);
    set e;
    set f;

    b.add_elements(5,13,23,4,101,761);
    c = b & a;
    d = a | b;
    e = a - b;
    f.add_elements(2,40,-20);
    print_set(a);
    print_set(b);
    print_set(c);
    print_set(d);
    print_set(e);
    print_set(f);
    printf("c has %d elements\n", c.size());
    printf("a.is_element(19)=%d\n", a.is_element(19));
    printf("a.is_element(33)=%d\n", a.is_element(33));
    c.make_empty();
    print_set(c);
    printf("c has %d elements\n", c.size());
    a.add_elements(10,0,73,89,-2,.\10,11,12,13,14,15);
    print_set(a); printf("a has %d elements\n", a.size());
    c = b;
    print_set(c);
    printf("c <= a = %d, c <= d = %d, c == d = %d\n",
           c <= a, c <= d, c == d);
    d &= a;
    f |= b;
    a -= b;
    print_set(a);
    print_set(d);
    print_set(f);

    return 0;
    }
```

2.
```
// complex.h - Definition of the class complex
// Defines a class which implements complex arithmetic

#include <math.h>

class complex {
 public:
    float x;  // Real part        z = x + iy
    float y;  // Imaginary part
```

```cpp
complex(float x1 = 0.0, float y1 = 0.0) {
      x = x1;
      y = y1;
      }

complex operator + (const complex & z2) const {
      complex temp(x + z2.x, y + z2.y);
      return temp;
      }

complex & operator += (const complex & z2) {
      x += z2.x;
      y += z2.y;
      return *this;
      }

complex operator - (const complex & z2) const {
      complex temp(x - z2.x, y - z2.y);
      return temp;
      }

complex & operator -= (const complex & z2) {
      x -= z2.x;
      y -= z2.y;
      return *this;
      }

complex operator * (const complex & z2) const {
      complex temp(x * z2.x - y * z2.y, y * z2.x + x * z2.y);
      return temp;
      }

complex & operator *= (const complex & z2) {
      float x1 = x;
      x = x*z2.x - y*z2.y;
      y = y*z2.x + x1*z2.y;
      return *this;
      }

complex operator / (const complex & z2) const {
      complex temp;
      float normsq = z2.x*z2.x + z2.y*z2.y;
      if (normsq > 0) {
            temp.x = (x * z2.x + y * z2.y) / normsq;
            temp.y = (y * z2.x - x * z2.y) / normsq;
            }
      return temp;
      }
```

```cpp
        complex & operator /= (const complex & z2) {
            float normsq = z2.x*z2.x + z2.y*z2.y;
            if (normsq > 0) {
                float x1 = x;
                x = (x*z2.x + y*z2.y) / normsq;
                y = (y*z2.x - x1*z2.y) / normsq;
                }
            return *this;
            }

        float norm() const {  // returns |z|
            return sqrt(x*x + y*y);
            }

        float arg() const {  // angle between z and real axis
            return atan2(y,x);
            }

        complex & polar2rect(float r, float theta) {
            // convert r*exp(i*theta) to a complex nbr in
            // rectangular form
            x = r*cos(theta);
            y = r*sin(theta);
            return *this;
            }

        int operator == (const complex & z2) const {
            return x == z2.x && y == z2.y;
            }

        int operator != (const complex & z2) const {
            return x != z2.x || y != z2.y;
            }

        void print(const char *prefix = "") const {
            printf("%s%g%+gi", prefix, x, y);
            return;
            }
};

/* test10-2.cpp - Program to test class complex */
/*  Chapter 10, exercise 2 */

#include <stdio.h>
#include "complex.h"

#define PRINT(z) z.print(" " #z "= ")
```

```
main()
{
    complex z1(2, -3), z2(-6, 9), z3(5), z4, z5, z6;
    PRINT(z1); PRINT(z2); PRINT(z3); PRINT(z4);
    putchar ('\n');

    z3 = z1 + z2;
    z4 = z1 - z2;
    z5 = z1 * z2;
    z6 = z1 / z2;
    PRINT(z3); PRINT(z4); PRINT(z5); PRINT(z6);
    putchar ('\n');

    z3 -= z2;   /* Should all be equal to z1 */
    z4 += z2;
    z5 /= z2;
    z6 *= z2;
    PRINT(z3); PRINT(z4); PRINT(z5); PRINT(z6);
    putchar('\n');

    printf("z1 == z2: %d, z1 != z2: %d\n", z1 == z2, z1 != z2);
    z2.polar2rect(z1.norm(), z1.arg());
    z3 = z1;
    PRINT(z1); PRINT(z2); PRINT(z3); putchar('\n');
    printf("z1 == z3: %d, z1 != z3: %d\n", z1 == z3, z1 != z3);

    printf("norm of z1 = %f, arg of z1 = %f\n", z1.norm(), z1.arg());
    return 0;
}
```

3.
```
// tuple.h - Definition of class n_tuple
// An n_tuple is an ordered list of N elements: [a1, a2, ...,aN]
// An n_tuple is implemented as an array with additional operations
// which allow lexicographical comparison of two n_tuples.

#include "array.h"

class n_tuple : public array {

 public:

    n_tuple(unsigned size = 1) : array(size) {}

    // copy constructor:
    n_tuple(const n_tuple & nt) : array(nt) {}

    // create an n_tuple with one or more elements:
    n_tuple(unsigned size, int element, ...);

    // use lexicographical ordering in the following
    // comparison operators
    int operator <= (const n_tuple &) const;
    int operator <  (const n_tuple &) const;
```

```cpp
        int operator >= (const n_tuple &nt) const {
         return nt.operator <= (*this);
          }
        int operator > (const n_tuple &nt) const {
         return nt.operator < (*this);
          }
        void print();
};

// tuple.cpp - Definition of member functions of class n_tuple

#include <stdio.h>
#include <stdarg.h>
#include "tuple.h"

#define TRUE 1
#define FALSE 0

// create an n_tuple with one or more elements:
n_tuple::n_tuple(unsigned size, int first, ...) : array(size)
{
    va_list ap;
    int element = first;
    int i;

    va_start(ap, first);
    for (i = 0; i < size; ++i) {
         (*this)[i] = element;
          element = va_arg(ap, int);
           }
    va_end(ap);
      }

// use lexicographical ordering in the following comparison operators
int n_tuple::operator <= (const n_tuple & nt) const
{
    unsigned i;
    unsigned min_size;
    if (size() == 0)
         return TRUE;
    if (nt.size() == 0)
         return FALSE;
    min_size = size() <= nt.size() ? size() : nt.size();

    for (i = 0; i < min_size; ++i) {
         if ((*this)[i] < nt[i])
              return TRUE;
         if ((*this)[i] > nt[i])
              return FALSE;
          }
     return size() <= nt.size();
      }
```

```cpp
int n_tuple::operator < (const n_tuple &nt) const
{
    unsigned i;
    unsigned min_size;
    if (nt.size() == 0)
        return FALSE;
    if (size() == 0)
        return TRUE;

    min_size = size() < nt.size() ? size() : nt.size();

    for (i = 0; i < min_size; ++i) {
        if ((*this)[i] < nt[i])
            return TRUE;
        if ((*this)[i] > nt[i])
            return FALSE;
    }
    return size() < nt.size();
}

void n_tuple::print()
{
    putchar('[');
    array::print();
    putchar(']');
    return;
}

// test10-3.cpp - Program to test class n_tuple

#include <stdio.h>
#include "tuple.h"

#define print_tuple(t)   printf(#t " = "); (t).print(); putchar('\n');

main()
{
    n_tuple t1(6,1,2,3,4,5,6);
    n_tuple t2(6,1,3,2,4,5,6);
    n_tuple t3 = t1;
    print_tuple(t1);
    print_tuple(t2);
    print_tuple(t3);
    printf("t1 <= t2: %d t1 < t2: %d\n", t1 <= t2);
    t3 = t2;
    print_tuple(t3)
    printf("t3 == t2: %d\n", t3 == t2);
    t3[2] = 1;
    print_tuple(t3);
}
```

REFERENCES

[Appleby, 1991]. Appleby, D. (1991). *Programming Languages: Paradigm and Practice*. New York: McGraw-Hill

[Feuer, 1982]. Feuer, Alan R. (1982). *The C Puzzle Book*. Englewood Cliffs, NJ: Prentice Hall.

[Plauger, 1989]. Plauger P. J. and Brodie Jim (1989) *Standard C: Programmer's Quick Refernce*. Redmond, Washington: Microsoft Press.

[Turbo, C88R]. (1988). *Turbo C: Reference Guide: Version 2.0*. Scotts Valley, CA: Borland International.

[Turbo, C88U]. (1988). *Turbo C: User's Guide: Version 2.0*. Scotts Valley, CA: Borland International.

INDEX

!= (not equal to) relational operator, 8, 96
#, for beginning preprocessor statements, 57, 58
#define statement
 for creating files, 59
 defining constants, 57–58
#include statement
 in C++, 73
 for file inclusion, 59
#undef statement, undefining names, 60
% (modulus) binary operator, 6–7, 95
% (percent sign), indicating a conversion specifier, 43
%d conversion specifier (int data type), 4
%d integer value conversion specification, 2
%f conversion specifier (float data type), 5
%f floating-point value conversion specification, 2
%hd conversion specifier (short int data type), 4
%hu conversion specifier (unsigned short data type), 4
%ld conversion specifier (long int data type), 4
%lf conversion specifier (double data type), 5
%Lf conversion specifier (long double data type), 5
%lu conversion specifier (unsigned long data type), 4
%o conversion specifier (octal values), 4
%u conversion specifier (unsigned data type), 4
%x conversion specifier (hexadecimal values), 4
& (address) operator, 2, 95
& (bitwise AND) binary bit operation, 9–10, 96
&& (AND) logical operator, 8, 96
() (parentheses), to indicate order of arithmetic operations, 2, 58, 95
* (asterisk), conversion specifier for the scanf library function, 45–46
* (multiply) binary operator, 6–7, 95
*/ (end of comment), 2
+ (add) binary operator, 6–7, 95
++ unary operator, 7
, (comma), in parameter lists, 36, 96
- (minus) unary operator, 7, 95
- (subtract) binary operator, 6–7, 95
-- unary operator, 7, 95
. (period) select member operator, 28, 95
/ (divide) binary operator, 6–7, 95
*/ (beginning of comment), 2
// (C++), indicating beginning of comment, 72
; (semicolon), indicating end of statement, 2
< (less than) relational operator, 8, 96
<< (left shift) binary bit operation, 9–10, 96
<= (less than or equal to) relational operator, 8, 96
= (equal) arithmetic operator, 7, 96
== (equal to) relational operator, 8
> (greater than) relational operator, 8, 96
>= (greater than or equal to) relational operator, 8, 96
>> (right shift) binary bit operation, 9–10, 96
\ (backslash), and the preprocessor, 58
\" (double quote) mnemonic, 6
\' (single quote) mnemonic, 6
\\ (backslash) mnemonic, 6
\f (formfeed) mnemonic, 6
\n (new line) mnemonic, 6
\t (tab) mnemonic, 6
^ (bitwise exclusive OR) binary bit operation, 9–10, 96
_ (underscore), indicating beginning of variable name, 3
| (bitwise inclusive OR) binary bit operation, 9–10, 96
|| (OR) logical operator, 8, 96
~ (bitwise NOT) unary bit operation, 9–10, 95

abs function, 97
absolute values, of numbers, 17
add (+) binary operator, 6–7, 95
address
 as the value of a pointer, 23
 of variables, 2
Add Watch command (Turbo C Break/Watch menu), 65
Alt-B (Turbo C hot key), 106
Alt-C (Turbo C hot key), 106
Alt-D (Turbo C hot key), 106
Alt-E (Turbo C hot key), 106

141

INDEX

Alt-F1 (Turbo C hot key), 106
Alt-F3 (Turbo C hot key), 106
Alt-F5 (Turbo C hot key), 63, 106
Alt-F6 (Turbo C hot key), 106
Alt-F7 (Turbo C hot key), 106
Alt-F8 (Turbo C hot key), 106
Alt-F9 (Turbo C hot key), 63, 106
Alt-F (Turbo C hot key), 106
Alt-O (Turbo C hot key), 106
Alt-P (Turbo C hot key), 106
Alt-R (Turbo C hot key), 106
Alt-X (Turbo C hot key), 106
AND (&&) logical operator, 8, 96
ANSI standard language description for C programming, 83–91
arithmetic data types, 3–6
arithmetic operations, order of, 2, 58
arithmetic operators
  binary, 6–7
  sample program illustrating, 9
  unary, 7
`array decoration` declaration syntax diagram, 88
arrays
  ascending, 81
  character strings as, 26
  general format, 24
  initializing, 26
  inserting and deleting data, 51
  multidimensional, 32
  passing to functions, 36
  two-dimensional, 32
ascending array, in a derived `class` (C++), 81
ASCII (American Standard Code for Information Interchange)
  characters, 6
  character set, 93–94
assignment operators, 7
asterisk (*), conversion specifier for the `scanf` library function, 45–46
`Auto Dependencies` command (Turbo C `Project` menu), 64

`auto` variable, 38
  sample program illustrating, 39

backslash (\), and the preprocessor, 58
backslash (\\) mnemonic, 6
beginning of comment (/*), 2
BEGIN (Pascal), 2
binary arithmetic operators, 6–7
binary bit operations, 9–10
binary difference operator (C++), in `class` fraction, 75
binary i/o, in i/o functions, 50
binary trees, 53–55
  illustrated model, 53
  See also linked lists
bit operations, 9–10
bitwise AND (&) binary bit operation, 9–10, 96
bitwise exclusive OR (^) binary bit operation, 9–10, 96
bitwise inclusive OR (|) binary bit operation, 9–10, 96
bitwise NOT (~) unary bit operation, 9–10, 95
`block` function definition syntax diagram, 90
blocks, 2
  defined, 13
  in function bodies, 37–38
Borland Turbo C++, xi. *See also* C++ programming language
Borland Turbo C Version 2.0, xi. *See also* Turbo C
`Break Make on` command (Turbo C `Project` menu), 64
breakpoints, in Turbo C, 65, 66
`break` statement, 15
  in loops, 18–19
Break/Watch menu (Turbo C), 65
  `Add Watch` command, 65
  `Clear All Breakpoint` command, 65
  `Delete Watch` command, 65
  `Edit Watch` command, 65

  `Remove All Watches` command, 65
  `Toggle Breakpoint` command, 65
  `View Next Breakpoint` command, 65
`Build All` command (Turbo C `Compile` menu), 64
built-in screen editor (Turbo C), 62

C++ programming language, 71–82
  classes, 71–73
  constructors, 74
  function prototypes, 75
  passing arguments by reference, 75
`calloc` function, 97
  in dynamic data structures, 55
case labels, of the `switch` statement, 15
case sensitivity, 3
character constants, 6
`character constant` token syntax diagram, 85
character graphics (Turbo C), 67
  `clrscr` function, 67, 97
  `gotoxy` function, 67, 100
  sample program illustrating, 68–69
  `wherex` function, 67, 104
  `wherey` function, 67, 104
characters, conversion specifiers for the `scanf` library function, 45–46
character strings, 26
  enumerated types, 26–28
  enumeration identifiers, 27–28
  sample program illustrating, 27
`char` (Character) data types, 6
  character strings, 26
  compatibility with `int` data types, 6
`class` array (C++)
  primary function, 79
  `protected` members, 79

INDEX 143

sample programs illustrating, 76, 78
See also classes (C++); `class` fraction (C++)
`class` constructor (C++), in a derived `class`, 79, 81
`class` data type (C++), 71–73
classes (C++), 71–73
  data hiding, 76
  derived `class`, 79–81
  encapsulation, 76
  inheritance, 76–77
  polymorphism, 76–77
  properties of, 76–77
  safe integer array, 77–78
  See also `class` array (C++); `class` fraction (C++)
`class` fraction (C++)
  definition, 72–73
  fraction operands, 74–75
  member functions, 74–76
  See also `class` array (C++); classes (C++)
`class` set (C++), 79–81
  sample program illustrating, 80
  subscript operator, 81
  See also `class` array (C++); classes (C++)
`Clear All Breakpoint` command (Turbo C `Break/Watch` menu), 65
`Clear Project` command (Turbo C `Project` menu), 64
`clrscr` function (Turbo C character graphics), 67, 97
comma (,), in parameter lists, 36, 96
command line arguments, and external files, 47–48
comments, 2
`Compile` menu (Turbo C), 63–64
  `Build All` command, 64
  `Compile to OBJ` command, 63
  `Get Info` command, 64
  `Link Exe File` command, 63
  `Make EXE FILE` command, 63
  `Primary C File` command, 64

`Compile to OBJ` command (Turbo C `Compile` menu), 63
compound statements, 13. *See also* blocks
conditional compilation
  as a debugging tool, 59–60
  and the preprocessor, 59–60
conditional expression operator, 17
constants
  character, 6
  defining, 57–58
  floating-point, 4–5, 8
`const` qualifier (C++), in `class` fraction, 75
constructors (C++), 74
`continue` statement, in loops, 19
control structures, 13–22
conversion specifications, 2, 4
conversion specifiers
  output, 45
  percent sign (%) indicating, 43
copy constructor (C++)
  in classes, 77
  default, 77
`cprintf` function, outputting to the window, 67
C programming language
  distinguished from other procedural languages, 23
  language description with syntax diagrams, 83–91
  references, 139
  sample program, 1–2
`cputs` function (Turbo C), outputting to the window, 67, 97
C tokens
  keywords listed, 83
  syntax diagrams, 84–85
Ctrl-F1 (Turbo C hot key), 105
Ctrl-F2 (Turbo C hot key), 63, 66, 105
Ctrl-F3 (Turbo C hot key), 105
Ctrl-F4 (Turbo C hot key), 64, 105
Ctrl-F7 (Turbo C hot key), 65, 105

Ctrl-F8 (Turbo C hot key), 105
Ctrl-F9 (Turbo C hot key), 63, 66, 105
cursor, moving in Turbo C, 62

data hiding (C++), in classes, 76
data structures
  allocating storage for, 51, 77
  dynamic, 51–55
data types
  of parameters, 36
  simple, 3–6
  synonyms for, 51–52
deallocation of memory, 77
`Debug/Evaluate` command (Turbo C Debug menu), 64
debugging
  in Turbo C, 65–66
  using conditional compilation, 59–60
Debug menu (Turbo C), 64
  `Debug/Evaluate` command, 64
`Debug/Source` Debugging toggle (Turbo C), 62–63
`declarations` syntax diagrams, 86–88
declaration syntax, syntax diagrams, 86–88
`declaration` syntax diagram, 86
`declarator` declaration syntax diagram, 87
`default` label, of the `switch` statement, 15
`Delete Watch` command (Turbo C `Break/Watch` menu), 65
denominator() member function (C++), 73, 74
derived `class` (C++), 79–81
  ascending array, 81
  print function, 81
destructor, for deallocating memory, 77
directories
  changing (Turbo C), 62
  displaying (Turbo C), 62
divide (/) binary operator, 6–7, 95

DOS, and i/o functions, 47
`double` data type, 4–5
   as the result of floating-point arithmetic, 8
double quote (`\"`) mnemonic, 6
`do-while` loop, 21
draw action (C++), of graphical objects, 77
dynamic data structures, 51–55
   binary trees, 52–55
   linked lists, 52
   sample program illustrating, 54–55

`Edit` command (Turbo C), 62
`Editor` commands (Turbo C), 62
`Edit Watch` command (Turbo C `Break/Watch` menu), 65
`Edit` window (Turbo C), 62
   entering code, 62
   insert mode, 62
encapsulation (C++), in classes, 76
end of comment (`*/`), 2
END (Pascal), 2
enumerated types of character strings, 26–28
enumeration identifiers of character strings, 27–28
EOF constant, 47, 48
equal to (`==`) relational operator, 8
escape sequences, 6
   conversion in i/o functions, 43
`escape sequence` token syntax diagram, 85
Euclid's algorithm, 20
`exit` function, 98
`expression` function definition syntax diagram, 90
expressions
   evaluation of, 58
   examining (Turbo C), 65
external files
   and command line arguments, 47–48
   and i/o functions, 47–49

F1 (Turbo C hot key), 105
F2 (Turbo C hot key), 61, 105
F3 (Turbo C hot key), 61, 105
F4 (Turbo C hot key), 62, 105
F5 (Turbo C hot key), 105
F6 (Turbo C hot key), 105
F7 (Turbo C hot key), 63, 65, 66, 105
F8 (Turbo C hot key), 63, 105
F9 (Turbo C hot key), 63, 105
F10 (Turbo C hot key), 62, 66, 105
`fclose` function, 98
   in i/o functions, 48–49
`feof` function, 98
Feuer, Alan, xi, 139
`fgetc` function, 98
`fgets` function, 98
   in i/o functions, 49
`File/Change Dir` option (Turbo C `File` menu), 62
`File/Directory` option (Turbo C `File` menu), 62
file inclusion, and the preprocessor, 59
`File/Load` option (Turbo C `File` menu), 61
`File` menu (Turbo C), 61–62
   `File/Change Dir` option, 62
   `File/Directory` option, 62
   `File/Load` option, 61
   `File/New` option, 61
   `File/OS Shell` option, 62
   `File/Pick` option, 61
   `File/Quit` option, 62
   `File/Save` option, 61
   `File/Write` option, 61
filenames, creating, 59
`File/New` option (Turbo C `File` menu), 61
FILE object type, 47
`File/OS Shell` option (Turbo C `File` menu), 62
`File/Pick` option (Turbo C `File` menu), 61
file pointers
   and i/o operations, 47
   references to streams, 43

`File/Quit` option (Turbo C `File` menu), 62
files
   combining multiple (Turbo C), 64
   loading (Turbo C), 61
   saving (Turbo C), 61
`File/Save` option (Turbo C `File` menu), 61
`File/Write` option (Turbo C `File` menu), 61
`float` data type, 4–5
   as the result of floating-point arithmetic, 8
`floating constant` token syntax diagram, 84
floating-point arithmetic, 8
floating-point constants, 4–5, 8
floating-point value conversion specification (`%f`), 2
floating (real) data types, 4–5
   sample program, 5
`float` variable, 2, 3
   as a return type in functions, 37
`fopen` function, 98
   and i/o functions, 47
`for` loop, 17–18
   nested, 18
`format` character string, 43
format strings, 2
formfeed (`\f`) mnemonic, 6
`fprintf` function, 99
   in i/o functions, 49
`fputc` function, 99
`fputs` function, 99
   in i/o functions, 49
fraction operands, in `class` fraction (C++), 74–75
`fread` function, in binary i/o functions, 50
`free` function, 99
`free` function (C++), for deallocating memory, 77
`fscanf` function, 99
   in i/o functions, 49
`fseek` function, 99
   in i/o functions, 49–50

F suffix (`float`), 5
`ftell` function, 100
   in i/o functions, 49–50
function bodies, 37–38
`function declaration` declaration syntax diagram, 88
`function definition` syntax diagram, 89
function parameters (C++), specification of default values, 74
function prototypes, 37
   in C++, 75
   header files, 37
functions, 35–42
   function bodies, 37–38
   function prototypes, 37
   general format, 35
   library functions, 35
   nonstatic, 39–40
   parameter lists, 36
   passing arrays to, 36
   recursive, 41–42
   return types, 37
   storage classes, 38–39
   as structure members (C++), 71
   See also individual functions
`fwrite` function, 100
   in binary i/o functions, 50

`gcd` member function (C++), 73
   of `class` fraction, 74
`getc` function, in i/o functions, 48
`getchar` library function, 100
   to input and output data, 43
   in standard i/o functions, 46–47
`Get Info` command (Turbo C `Compile` menu), 64
`gets` function, 100
   in standard i/o functions, 46–47
global variables, 38–39
   sample program illustrating, 41
   See also variables

`Go to Cursor` command (Turbo C `Run` menu), 63
`goto` statement, in loops, 21
`gotoxy` function (Turbo C character graphics), 67, 100
greater than (>) relational operator, 8, 96
greater than or equal to (>=) relational operator, 8, 96

header files
   file inclusion, 59
   and nonstatic functions, 39–40
   standard, 43, 52
   system, 59
hexadecimal integer constants, 4
hexadecimal values of the ASCII character set, 93–94
hot keys (Turbo C), 61–66, 105–106

identifiers, in statements, 21
`if-else` statement, 13–14
   indentation, 15
`if` statement, 13
   nested, 14–15
`include` directive, 43, 73
`infix operator` function definition syntax diagram, 91
inheritance (C++), in object-oriented programming, 76–77
`init` member function (C++), 73
   of `class` fraction, 74
`inline` functions (C++), 73
input/output (i/o). *See* i/o (input/output) functions
insert mode, in the Turbo C `Edit` window, 62
integer arithmetic, 7–8
integer constants, octal and hexadecimal, 4
`integer constant` token syntax diagram, 84
integer (`int`) data type. *See* `int` (integer) data type
integer value conversion specification (%d), 2
integrated debugger (Turbo C), 64, 65–66

`int` (integer) data type, 4
   compatibility with `char` data type, 6
   converting to `long` in `class` fraction (C++), 75
   `long` modifier, 4
   in parameter lists, 37
   as the result of an integer expression, 8
   `short` modifier, 4
`int` (integer) variable, 2, 3
i/o (input/output) functions, 43–50
   binary i/o, 50
   random access to files, 49–50
   standard i/o, 43–47
   using external files, 47–49
`isalnum` function, 100
`isdigit` function, 100–101
ISO standard language description for C programming, 83–91
`isspace` function, 101

keywords, listed, 83

labels, in statements, 21
language description for C programming, with syntax diagrams, 83–91
leaves, defined, 54
left shift (<<) binary bit operation, 9–10, 96
less than (<) relational operator, 8, 96
less than or equal to (<=) relational operator, 8, 96
library functions, 35. *See also individual library functions*
linked lists, 52
   binary trees, 52–55
   inserting nodes, 53
   See also dynamic data structures
`Link Exe File` command (Turbo C `Compile` menu), 63
lists, linked, 52, 53

local variables, and parameter lists, 36. *See also* variables
`log10` function, 101
`log` function, 101
logical operators, 8–9, 96
  sample program illustrating, 9
`long` data type
  in `class` fraction (C++), 75
  as the result of an integer expression, 8
`long double` data type, 4–5
  as the result of floating-point arithmetic, 8
`long` modifier, `int` (integer) data type, 4
looping constructs, 17–21
loop statements, terminating, 15
lowercase letters, 3
L suffix (`long double`), 5

macro definitions, 57–58
macros
  advantages over functions, 58
  disadvantages of, 58
`main` function, 2, 35, 39
Make EXE FILE command (Turbo C `Compile` menu), 63
`malloc` function, 101
  in linked lists, 52
`memcmp` function, 101
`memmove` function, 101
memory address. *See* address
memory allocation
  in creating arrays (C++), 77
  for data structures, 51
  deallocation, 77
`memset` function, 102
menus, Turbo C, 61–65
minus (-) unary operator, 7
mnemonics, in escape sequences, 6
modules
  compiling, 40
  grouping functions into files, 39
  and project files, 40
modulus (%) binary operator, 6–7, 95

multidimensional arrays, 32. *See also* arrays
multiply (*) binary operator, 6–7, 95

names
  undefining, 60
  of variables, 3
`name` token syntax diagram, 83, 84
nested `if` statement, 14–15
newline character, 6
new line (\n) mnemonic, 6
nodes
  inserting in linked lists, 53
  in linked lists, 52
  without branches, 54
nonstatic functions, 39–40
not equal to (!=) relational operator, 8, 96
NULL constant
  in i/o functions, 49
  in linked lists, 52
numbers, absolute values of, 17
numerator() member function (C++), 73, 74

object-oriented programming (OOP), 71. *See also* C++ programming language
objects (C++), 71
  properties of, 76
octal integer constants, 4
octal values of the ASCII character set, 93–94
OOP (object-oriented programming), 71. *See also* C++ programming language
`operator -` functions (C++), in `class` fraction, 75
`operator long` member function (C++), in `class` fraction, 75
`operator` member function (C++), in `class` fraction, 75
operator precedence, 95–96
operators, valid, 86
`opt` function definition syntax diagram, 90

Options menu (Turbo C), 64
OR (||) logical operator, 8, 96
output conversion specifiers, 45
output. *See* i/o (input/output) functions
overload operator, in `class` array (C++), 79

parameter lists, 36
parameters (C++), specification of default values, 74
parameters types, specified by function prototypes, 37
parentheses (()), to indicate order of arithmetic operations, 2, 58, 95
Pascal programming language, 2
percent sign (%), indicating a conversion specifier, 43
period (.) select member operator, 28, 95
pointer arithmetic, sample program illustrating, 25
`pointer decoration` declaration syntax diagram, 88
pointers, 23–25
  file pointers, 43
  general format, 23
  as parameters, 36
  value of, 23
polymorphism (C++), in object-oriented programming, 76–77
`postfix operator` function definition syntax diagram, 91
postincrement operators, 7
`prefix operator` function definition syntax diagram, 91
preincrement operators, 7
preprocessor, 57–60
  conditional compilation, 59–60
  file inclusion, 59
  macro definitions, 57–58
preprocessor directives, 2
preprocessor statements, beginning, 57

INDEX 147

`Primary C File` command (Turbo C `Compile` menu), 64
`printf` library function, 2, 35, 102
 conversion specifics for, 44–45
 formatting output, 43
 to input and output data, 43
print function
 in `class` array (C++), 81
 in a derived `class` (C++), 81
`private` keyword (C++), 73
procedural languages, C compared to other, 23
`Program Reset` command (Turbo C `Run` menu), 63
project files, and module names, 40
ProjectMake facility, 40
`Project` menu (Turbo C), 64
 `Auto Dependencies` command, 64
 `Break Make on` command, 64
 `Clear Project` command, 64
 `Project Name` command, 64
 `Remove Messages` command, 64
`Project Name` command (Turbo C `Project` menu), 64
`protected` members (C++), of `class` array, 79
`public` qualifier (C++), in `class` array, 79
`putc` function, in i/o functions, 48
`putchar` function, 102
`puts` function, 102
 in standard i/o functions, 46–47

random access to files, in i/o functions, 49–50
real (floating-point) numbers, 4–5
records, sample program illustrating, 30–31
records (Pascal), 28
recursion, 41–42

`reduce` member function (C++), 73
reference, as an alias for another variable, 74
relational operators, 8
 sample program illustrating, 9
remainders, in integer arithmetic, 7
`Remove All Watches` command (Turbo C `Break/Watch` menu), 65
`Remove Messages` command (Turbo C `Project` menu), 64
`return` statement (C++), and constructors, 74
return types, of functions, 37
right shift (>>) binary bit operation, 9–10, 96
`Run` menu (Turbo C), 62–63
 `Go to Cursor` command, 63
 `Program Reset` command, 63
 `Run/Run` command, 63
 `Step Over` command, 63
 `Trace Into` command, 63
 `User Screen` command, 63
`Run/Run` command (Turbo C `Run` menu), 63

safe integer array (C++), in classes, 77–78
`scanf` library function, 2, 35, 102
 conversion specifiers for, 46
 to input and output data, 43
 in i/o functions, 45–46
screen, directing output to (Turbo C), 67
semicolon (;), indicating end of statement, 2
Shift-F10 (Turbo C hot key), 105
`short` modifier, `int` (integer) data type, 4
sign bits, of floating (real) data types, 4
`signed` data type, 4
single quote (\') mnemonic, 6
`sizeof` operator, 31, 95
`sprintf` function, 102
`sqrt` function, 103

`sscanf` function, 103
standard header file, 43. *See also* header files
standard i/o, 43–47. *See also* i/o (input/output) functions
`statement` function definition syntax diagram, 89
statements, end of, 2
`static` variable, 38
 and global variables, 38
 sample program illustrating, 39
`stddef.h` standard header file, 52
`stderr` (error output) file pointer, 43
`stdin` (standard input) file pointer, 43
 and external files, 47
`stdio.h` standard header file, 43
`stdlib.h` header file, in dynamic data structures, 55
`stdout` (standard output) file pointer, 43
 and external files, 47
`Step Over` command (Turbo C `Run` menu), 63
storage allocation, for data structures, 51, 77
storage classes, 38–39
`strcat` library function, 103
 for use with strings, 26
`strcmp` function, 103
`strcpy` library function, 28, 35, 103
streams, and i/o functions, 43
`string literal` token syntax diagram, 85
strings, conversion specifiers for the `scanf` library function, 45–46. *See also* character strings
`strlen` function, 103
`strncat` function, 103
`strncmp` function, 104
`strncpy` function, 104
`struct` (structure) data type, 28–29
 as a node in a linked lists, 52

structured programming, principle of, 21
structures, 28–29
 defining an array of, 28–29
 dynamic data structures, 51–55
 general format, 28
 name, 28
subscript operator
 in class array (C++), 79
 in class set (C++), 81
subtract (-) binary operator, 6–7, 95
switch statement, 15–16
 sample program illustrating, 16
syntax diagrams for C programming, 84–91
system header files, 59

tab (\t) mnemonic, 6
TC hot keys, 61–66, 105–106
term function definition syntax diagram, 90
this keyword (C++), in a derived class, 81
Toggle Breakpoint command (Turbo C Break/Watch menu), 65
tolower function, 104
toupper function, 104
Trace Into command (Turbo C Run menu), 63
translation unit declaration syntax diagram, 86
Turbo C++ (Borland), xi
Turbo C, 61–69
 Break/Watch menu, 65
 built-in screen editor, 62
 character graphics, 67, 68–69
 combining multiple files, 64
 Compile menu, 63–64
 controlling breakpoints, 65
 controlling watch expressions, 65
 Debug menu, 64

directing output to the screen, 67
Edit command, 62
Editor commands, 62
ending debugging sessions, 62, 66
File menu, 61–62
menus, 61–65; toggling between, 61
Options menu, 64
Project menu, 64
quitting, 62
references, 139
Run menu, 62–63
running programs, 62
tailoring the environment, 64
TC hot keys, 61–66, 105–106
using the debugger, 64, 65–66
Version 2.0 (Borland), xi
window function, 67
Turbo C Editor, 65–66
two-dimensional arrays, 32. See also arrays
type cast operators, 10–11
typedef variable, 51–52
type part declaration syntax diagram, 87

unary arithmetic operators, 7
unary bit operation, 9–10
unary minus operator (C++), in class fraction, 75, 95
undefining names, 60
underscore (_), indicating beginning of variable name, 3
unions, 29–31
 general format, 29
 name, 29
 sample program illustrating, 30–31
UNIX, and i/o functions, 47
unsigned data type, 4
unsigned int data type, as the result of an integer expression, 8

unsigned long data type, as the result of an integer expression, 8
uppercase letters, 3
User Screen command (Turbo C Run menu), 63

valid operators, listed, 86
value declaration syntax diagram, 88
variable declarations, 2
variable names, 3
 valid and invalid, 3
variables, 2
 address, 2
 auto, 38
 changing values with pointers, 24
 examining (Turbo C), 65
 global, 38–39
 local, 36
 names, 3
 references as aliases for, 74
 static, 38
 swapping, 36
 types, 2, 3
variant records (Pascal), 29
View Next Breakpoint command (Turbo C Break/Watch menu), 65
virtual qualifier (C++), in class array, 81
void data type
 in functions, 37
 in parameter lists, 37

wherex function (Turbo C character graphics), 67, 104
wherey function (Turbo C character graphics), 67, 104
while loop, 19–20
 sample program, 20
window function (Turbo C), 67
windows
 changing active, 67
 defined, 67
 outputting to, 67